the Unofficial Guide® to Flipping Properties

Peter A. Richmond

1807
WILEY
2007

Wiley Publishing, Inc.

Library of Congress Control Number: 2006034743

ISBN: 978-0-471-79910-8

Manufactured in the United States of America

10 9 8 7 6 5 4 3 2

Book design by Melissa Auciello-Brogan
Page creation by Wiley Publishing, Inc. Composition Services

To my wife, Jane, who has encouraged my writing from the start and been a real source of support as I've "followed my muse." Whenever I've needed support or unvarnished opinion of a word or phrase, she has been there to provide it. Thank you for all of your patience, support, understanding, and, most important, love and kindness.

To my two wonderful daughters, Jenn and Sara. They are all of the inspiration that any father ever needs in pursuing his dreams. Jenn's writing sets a wonderful example for this dad, and Sara's will and inner strength will change the world. Thank you for your encouragement and the joy of watching you both as you grow in your lives.

To my parents, without whom I wouldn't be here. Though they are both gone, it is their values, loving guidance, and teaching that has made me the person that I am, and for that I am truly forever grateful.

Finally, to Adair Lara, a wonderful writer and great teacher, and my writers' group; you all have taught me many valuable lessons that I hope make my writing instructive and enjoyable to all who read it. Thanks—I hope you enjoy the results.

Acknowledgments

I'd like to thank Melissa Prandi for introducing me to my agent, Marilyn Allen, and for Marilyn's introduction to Pam Mouzouris, the Acquisitions Editor at Wiley Publishing. Pam's review and testing of my abilities helped to make this a successful experience.

Thank you to my wonderful project editor, Lynn Northrup, for all of your patience, ideas, and professionalism in making this book what I hope will become a true sourcebook on the art of flipping houses. Lynn, you are a great source of assistance and very much appreciated.

Thank you to all of those who gave of their time and energy, Robert Kleiner, Alan Garber, Cindy Anderson, and Retie Brown, in reviewing portions of the book and offering their ideas and suggestions as we proceeded. Thank you, too, to friends, colleagues, and assorted experts in the field who willingly gave me good ideas and commentary as the book developed. Tami Gendel, Christine Pang, Megan Clark, and Marie Kuykendall— you all are terrific.

I also want to thank my accountant, Jack Vogensen, who lent his assistance and advice on the tax implication information in the book.

Finally, I want to thank my friends and associates for all of their encouragement, support, and understanding as we proceeded from concept to completion of this book. It is appreciated.

Contents

Peter A. Richmond is a Realtor with Pacific Union Real Estate in Mill Valley, California. He has worked in real estate for 13 years, following a 25-year career in international banking and finance that included assignments to Germany, England, and Pakistan.

Peter represents clients in both residential and commercial real estate, working with his wife, Jane, at Pacific Union. He is a member of the Allen F. Hainge Cyberstars, and is a recognized expert on the purchase and sale of foreclosed properties.

Peter's leisure activities include skiing, cycling, and martial arts, in which he holds a second-degree black belt in Tae Kwon Do.

He and Jane live in Mill Valley, where he is currently working on his second novel.

This book is about the process in real estate that has come to be known as "flipping." Simply put, flipping involves the purchase, rehabilitation or remodeling, and sale of a particular piece of real property. As you shall see in these chapters, there is really no limitation to the types of property and related reconstructions that can be flipped. Any seeming limits as we proceed will be solely for the purpose of making the process a bit more understandable and easy to follow.

You may want to ask yourself a couple of questions before getting too deeply involved in the practice of flipping properties. First, why do you want to consider doing a flip? If it's just a whim, and you have no reason beyond that, you probably should stop right now and do some careful thinking about exactly why you want to flip and what your goals are. Simply saying that you intend to make a lot of money at it is not enough.

Perhaps you've bought and sold property as a part of your investment activity over the years and have finally decided to take on a new way to profit at real estate, hopefully one that will increase your return on the equity you invest, and in a shorter amount of time. Maybe you did a flip a while ago and for any number of reasons have decided that it's time to attempt another.

Maybe your normal source of income is construction or arranging for construction financing. But, up to now, you've always worked on or financed someone else's projects. You've carefully observed the procedure and have decided that you'd like to try to put your efforts into something that will benefit you for a change.

Perhaps you know someone who has done a few flips and benefited from the results. You've analyzed that individual's history, possibly even talked with him or her, and decided that this is something you want to try. Whatever the reason, you have decided to consider doing a flip.

The next thing to consider is how this ranks for you as an investment. Just as with any investment, flipping properties has its own unique risks and rewards, and you should consider them all before moving forward. Ask yourself, "Are there any better or less risky types of investments that will produce a similar return on the money I'm about to invest?" There may be, but even if there are a few, you may still decide you want to try flipping. That's fine. The next thing to do is to consider your appetite for the risk involved, as compared with the risk involved in any other type of investment you'd normally contemplate. If, after all this contemplation, you still wish to undertake a flip, great! This book will tell you everything you need to know. Now, let's get the process underway.

What This Book Offers You

The Unofficial Guide to Flipping Properties will help you get the "inside scoop" on the best—and most profitable—ways to flip houses, from simply adding a little fresh paint to totally gutting and rebuilding a house.

By reading this *Unofficial Guide,* you will get:

- Information on how to locate and assess properties that are suitable for flipping.

- The inside scoop on budgeting to ensure your flip will be profitable.

- Details about potential problems and how to solve them.

- A description of the planning necessary to make a project successful.

- The latest data on the importance of seller disclosure.

- Important information about proper construction scheduling.

- A clear explanation of the best and cheapest methods of financing.

- Recent research on the value of staging houses to receive more money from buyers.

- Detailed information on tax considerations that can help you keep more of your profits.

Special Features

Every book in the *Unofficial Guide* series offers the following four special sidebars that are devised to help you get things done cheaply, efficiently, and smartly.

1. **Moneysaver:** Tips and shortcuts that will help you save money.

2. **Watch Out!:** Cautions and warnings to help you avoid common pitfalls.

3. **Bright Idea:** Smart or innovative ways to do something; in many cases, the ideas listed here will help you save time or hassle.

4. **Quote:** Anecdotes from real people who are willing to share their experiences and insights.

We also recognize your need to have quick information at your fingertips, and have provided the following comprehensive sections at the back of the book:

1. **Glossary:** Definitions of complicated terminology and jargon.

2. **Resource Guide:** Lists of relevant Web sites and computer programs.

3. **Recommended Reading List:** Suggested titles that can help you get more in-depth information on related topics.

4. **Words of Wisdom:** Ideas and commentary from experienced flippers.

5. **Before and After:** Before-and-after photos of a typical intermediate flip. It's hard to believe it's the same house!

6. **Index.**

Initial Decisions

PART I

GET THE SCOOP ON...
To flip or not to flip? ▪ How to determine an
investment's profitability ▪ Looking at non-flip
real estate investments ▪ How to calculate ROI ▪
Rule number one: Use someone else's money

Establishing Your Goals

A s with anything in which you invest your time and money, flipping a property involves a number of basic requirements before you even begin. The most important of these are:

▪ Determine your goals

▪ Make sure of your project or investment's profitability

▪ Compare the desired return on investment (ROI) of your project with that of competing non-real estate investments

There are probably other pre-investment admonitions to consider in any investment, but, when considering a flip, these three are the most important. The reasons for this are simple. Knowing what your goals are will go a long way toward helping you decide whether this is a one-time thing or the start of a fairly regular activity on your part. It will also help you decide how deeply you wish to become involved on a project-by-project basis. Will you stick to cosmetic fixes or get involved in projects that require more time, energy, and money? (I cover these different types of projects in detail in Chapters 3, 10, 11, and 12.)

3

Should you flip?

If the project doesn't appear likely to yield a profit, there is no sense in even beginning it. After all, why become involved if not for a return on the time and money you'll be investing in the project? Flipping a property without regard to its profitability is *not*, by itself, sufficient reason to do a flip.

Equally important, even if you are certain that your project will return a profit, it still may not be the best use of your funds. Perhaps there is another type of investment in or outside real estate that will result in a better return on your investment than the flip you are considering. It might be some form of real estate investment such as buying foreclosed properties and then immediately selling them at market value, or it could be investing in real estate investment trusts, better known as REITs. It might be stocks and bonds, collectibles, or an assortment of commodities.

Also, the competing real estate or non-real estate investments you might consider may bring you a higher ROI than your proposed flip without entailing the same level of risk. In the alternative, they may bring a slightly lower ROI than your project, but with a great deal less risk, so you may yet decide that there is a better place for your money than in redoing an old house.

It is important to remember that whereas many other types of investments are passive, a real estate flip is anything but. It requires a great deal of time and effort, the value of which, if quantifiable, should also be entered into the ROI equation.

Finally, there is the philosophical question of what we choose to do with our lives. Turning a sow's ear of a property into a silk purse of a house can be very satisfying and that could be worth a few percentage points of profit to some people.

Assessing profitability

"All right," you respond. "So how do I determine whether or not my project is likely to return a profit? And, assuming it appears that it will, how detailed should my comparison be with other investment vehicles?" The answer to these questions is *simple*.

You will be able to determine its likely profitability by *carefully* analyzing the real estate market for such properties, the economy, and costs involved in the process of doing a flip. The cost analysis of the project will include a detailed budget of every single item or expense involved in the project, as well as a few items you might not have thought of if you're relatively new to the game. The following chapters will provide you with a much more detailed guide to doing your profitability investigation.

When comparing your project's ROI to that of other competing investments, in or out of real estate, the depth of investigation you undertake is your own decision. It may be that you've arbitrarily decided on a certain rate of return as satisfactory for your project, regardless of the ROIs of competing places for your money, or you may have decided that if you can yield a certain minimum amount of profit in dollars before tax you'll be satisfied. In that case, your investigation won't likely be as in-depth as it might otherwise be without these predeterminations. Just remember, be as detailed as possible within the scope of your project and your desired ROI. More time spent here can avoid a great deal of worry and unhappiness later in the project.

On the assumption that you haven't made a specific percent or dollar determination as your goal, your comparison will be done by calculating your project's ROI and comparing it against whatever other types of investments have shown in the recent past as their respective ROIs. If, for example, gold has an ROI over a six-month period of 20 percent, and you can stomach its wild fluctuation potential, it may be a better investment than your project if your project will yield only 15 percent ROI.

On the other hand, if you are comparing ROIs with growth stocks and they yield an average of 12 percent, your projected hypothetical 15 percent ROI may indicate that your project is currently the better investment.

You can do a similar comparison with any number of potentially competing investments. But be careful: With the exception of U.S. government debt instruments (Treasury Bills and

Watch Out!

So-called growth stocks, although given to fairly high rates of growth, and thus, good ROI, have a tendency to be among the ones most likely to fluctuate wildly in both directions, thus potentially risking a negative or lower ROI if you decide to, or find you must, cash them in at a certain point.

Notes); there is no instrument that I am aware of whose return can be relied upon 100 percent. Whatever the stated interest rate payable on these instruments is, that is the amount you will receive. From there it is very easy to calculate your ROI, and know with certainty that you will receive that specific ROI. All other types of investments can wax and wane as to both value and rate of return on your investment.

Non-flip real estate investments

Another type of competing investment worth considering is a basic non-flip real estate investment. This is the traditional type where the investor buys a property, (residential or commercial—it makes no difference for the purposes of our analysis), rents it out, and, if he or she has planned well, eventually sells it at a profit. The investor's profit at sale will then be used to calculate the ROI of that particular investment. A slight variation on this theme is to purchase foreclosed property, either at auction or from the foreclosing lender, and then either retain it as a rental or immediately turn around and sell it at market value, presumably more than you just paid to acquire it.

Calculating ROI

As simple as it is to calculate ROI, there is often confusion about how to do it. Your ROI is the percentage of your original investment that is returned to you when you sell it. If, for example, you invest $100,000 of your own money into an investment, and you ultimately sell it with a net profit before taxes of $25,000, you have achieved an ROI of 25 percent. That profit you received for your efforts is what's left above and beyond the funds you received that covered your original investment, as well as, in the case of a flip, all of the costs involved in successfully completing the project.

If you invested the same $100,000 as a down payment on the property you intended to flip, along with a loan from the bank of $300,000 that covered not only the balance of the purchase, but also the costs of improving the property before sale, you have still only invested $100,000. The other $300,000 was not your investment. It was money you borrowed to allow you to complete your project. In effect, it was as much a tool as a hammer or table saw. Like these obvious tools, it was a necessary item to complete the project into which you invested your $100,000. Therefore, your ROI is calculated on the investment you made, in this case, $100,000, *not* the total initial cost to you before sale. Therefore, if you were to ultimately sell this property for $500,000, your profit would be $100,000, but your ROI would *not* be 25 percent. It would actually be 100 percent, as it is the percent return on *your* investment, your original seed capital, in this case, of $100,000.

Using someone else's money

Another word of advice is worthwhile at this point: No successful real estate investor, and I mean *no one,* ever got rich by using only his or her own money. The rule, virtually etched in stone, is to use someone else's money to as large a degree as you can, and still have it make sense in your overall budget and plan. If things go south and you lose a large portion of your cost invested, the smaller the portion of the funds expended that is actually your money, the less you actually have to lose.

 Watch Out!

The costs of the loan, such as interest, closing costs, and points, must be added to the expense of doing the project when estimating your ROI.

Bright Idea

Use leverage (borrowed funds) to as large a degree as possible, within reason. Borrowing can be from banks or personal acquaintances such as relatives or friends.

There are two exceptions to this general rule. If you are a first-time flipper it may be hard to get someone else's money. Also, if you already have the liability of a mortgage on your own home, then an additional loan for your flip can be difficult to get.

Just the facts

- Once you have done as much comparison and analysis as you feel is necessary, make your decision—flip or don't flip.

- Before you invest any time or money in flipping a property, consider how profitable your investment is likely to be.

- Look at all the potential risks, benefits, and any other factors that could affect that investment's projected ROI, for better or worse.

- Consider a non-flip real estate investment, in which you buy a property, rent it out, and then sell it at a profit.

- As much as is practical, use borrowed funds.

GET THE SCOOP ON...
Assessing the state of the market ▪ Studying the
economy ▪ Demographic indicators ▪ Government
help or hindrance ▪ Picking someone else's brains

Doing Your Research

Research: It's one of the most important parts of successfully flipping a property. It is just as important to the success of the project as the architect's drawings, your financing plans for the flip, the materials you'll be using, or the actual labor in assembling them into the finished product. The reason is simple. Without the proper research, you'll have no idea whatsoever if your project fits the market, can be done profitably, or can be built as you think you'd like it to be. More important, your research can indicate if you should even do a flip at the present time or under the present market conditions. It can not only provide you valuable information necessary to make that project a total success, but it can also help you avoid making a very large and potentially very costly mistake.

Your research will include a close examination of a number of widely diverse subjects and items. You'll consider such issues as the health of the overall economy, what inflation looks like and is expected to do over the planned time of your project, as well as the Gross Domestic Product, or GDP. Obviously, if the

Chapter 2

9

economy is either mired in the depths of a major recession or is expected to head in that direction, it is probably not a good time to undertake anything as involved and expensive as a flip.

How's the market?

Starting from scratch, your obvious first question is, "How's the local real estate market where I'm considering a flip?" Answer it after checking the following sources and subjects. The logical first group with whom to discuss the subject is your local Realtors. They will know better than anyone else exactly what is happening in the local real estate market. Are homes selling or not, for how much, and of what type? What are the best neighborhoods, what are the most desired things buyers are seeking, and how long are homes taking to sell? All of this information can be obtained gratis from your local Realtor where your undertaking is located. The agent will also be able to tell you what you can expect to receive when you sell your completed venture, based on the current comps in that market and the projections of where the market is expected to go in the next year or so. ("Comps" are the actual similar properties in the same area that either have recently sold or are currently on the market.) These projections should be on the market in general, as well as the market for the specific type of project you envision doing.

Economic considerations

If inflation is climbing rapidly, it may be a good time to do a flip, assuming the rest of the economy, including salaries, is following suit. On the other hand, if inflation is climbing and the Federal

Bright Idea

Obviously, the Realtor you may be using to help find the home you plan to flip will be a major source of information. However, there is nothing stopping you from also chatting with other Realtors, either at their offices, on the phone, by e-mail, or at open houses they may be holding that you visit during your search for the "right" property.

Watch Out!

Rising inflation may cause interest rates to rise to a level that precludes doing a project that will be profitable.

Reserve is tightening the screws on interest rates, causing them, along with your costs, to increase as well, it could punch a large hole in the side of your project. This will either make it difficult for you to sell at a profit, or completely preclude your ability to finance the development of the building, much less get it sold at completion.

If the overall economy is robust—and, even better, expected by the experts to remain that way for the next year or two—it is likely an excellent time to proceed on a flip. If the economy is healthy, it follows that the buying market you'll be appealing to will also be in a good position to respond favorably to what you are producing. In this type of economy, jobs are usually more plentiful, salaries are generally on the increase, the per-capita rates of disposable income are climbing, and people, in general, are optimistic about the economy and therefore more likely to be interested in a major purchase such as a house.

Looking at demographics

Another area to closely examine in your research is that of demographics. Demographics are the use of statistics to determine economic and social trends. It makes use of information about what's happening in a society and economy to determine in what direction those things are likely to continue moving. You will want to consider changes in the size of the population, actual and projected, in the locale where you are working. Clearly, you won't be inspired to get very deeply involved in a flip if the projected population is expected to drop markedly. Conversely, if the population is growing, and projected to continue to do so, it would seem like an excellent point in time to do a flip, and, if successful, another after that.

Watch Out!

Be certain your information is more than just the "first rumor" of corporate decisions. Try to get more than one corroborating source.

Along with trends in population, you should look at reasons why the population is changing. Are there major corporate changes underway? Has one or more large firms announced either expansion in your area, or, conversely, a downsizing of its operation? Right in hand with corporate activity is the category of income growth. Is it increasing or decreasing where you are, and what are the trends in the area for the next year or two? Maybe there is some corporate expansion in your area, but most of it is blue collar. That set of facts could indicate flips are a good idea, but only if limited to the economic strata involved in the income growth. With such a set of circumstances, you'd likely concentrate on flips that were basic homes, perhaps on a cosmetic level, instead of getting involved in high-end homes and total guts (see Chapter 12). A good example of this type of activity occurs when a major manufacturing firm decides to open a new manufacturing plant in a particular area and mentions as part of its announcement that 95 percent of the jobs the establishment of that plant will create are assembly line, rather than executive. Right away, you know that there will be a market for houses for a specific level of income, and can plan your project based, at least in part, on that set of facts.

Conversely, if a company announces a new research center, or the expansion of an existing one, with the bulk of the positions to be held by high-income research types, you'll be able to factor in this information, and perhaps attempt a more involved or more expensive undertaking.

Government information

The sources of this type of information are as varied as the types of information making it up. You should include local and state chambers of commerce, as well as trade and industry groups where particular industries are clustered. Government offices are also available to assist in this kind of research. At all levels, from federal to municipal, commerce departments, or their equivalents, collect and disseminate such information, frequently for the asking. Foreign consulates or embassies may also be a source if the expanding firm is a foreign-owned one.

An additional source of governmental information may sometimes come in the form of a particular level of government's office promoting inward investment. Usually, these are on the state level, but there are also sometimes local city offices involved in the same type of activity. What these agencies do is simple: They encourage corporate investment in their particular locale, using cash grants, low-interest loans, reduced taxes or tax holidays, or some combination of these items as a method of persuasion. That new automotive assembly plant or computer-chip wafer fabrication facility you just heard about that's coming next year to your state didn't just happen. Chances are there was some heavy financial arm-twisting that preceded it by the local government concerned, and against similar activity from any number of competing locales. The reason for this was to generate a stronger local economy, a larger tax base, and all of the benefits, real and imagined, that follow from such an event.

Other sources of demographic information include the local library, newspapers, and electronic media. Whenever a company announces a major decision on its size, good or bad, it shows up in the newspapers of the region or city affected, and is also reported by television and on the Internet. In many cases, the press releases will be quite detailed as to numbers of jobs involved, and, possibly, the total amount of money to be spent or saved by the company making the announcement. Sometimes your local Realtor can direct you to such announcements. This type of announcement is valuable to you because it is "solid" intelligence on a major event that will definitely affect the market you're considering for your flip.

Moneysaver

Your Web research can save money by giving you info for free that you might otherwise have to pay substantial money to a consultant to obtain. It also will save you time, which is always valuable.

I mentioned the Internet as a source of information. You can use this tool to research virtually all of the types of information I'm discussing in this chapter. Do a search on the locale through Web sites of the local governing body, the chamber of commerce, or the site of the firm or firms you find have made announcements about their plans for their operations in the area. You may find that your use of the Web will also give you some leads to additional sources of information that will be very valuable to you in your analysis.

I recently concluded an acquisition of a piece of property in the Pacific Northwest, partly based on projections of major expansion by a Fortune 500 company with large facilities located in the area. While only time will tell if those projections, and my investment, bear out, the projected growth from the operations of that firm, and their economic "throw-off," were one of the reasons I chose that locale.

Government activity

Another demographic to closely consider is what I call government or infrastructure activity. What is being done by the responsible government/agency regarding local infrastructure components? Are new highways, government offices, schools, airports, and public transit facilities being added to an area? Conversely, are they and/or the services provided being reduced or sold off? Do the existing public facilities appear largely in good condition, or are they aging and in serious need of repair or replacement? If major infrastructure expenditure is underway, it is a sign that would certainly favor the locale for your project(s).

In the area of governmental growth, new policies or pro-grams by government may be the basis for a surge in population and, thus, the demand for housing. For example, in 2005, California announced the commencement of stem cell research, headquartered in the San Francisco area. If the pro-ject grows enough, it could mean there will be a demand for increased housing for the scientists and researchers who move to the area.

Similarly, the federal government created the Bureau of Homeland Security to coordinate the nation's efforts to increase domestic security. Depending on the geographic loca-tion of any growth associated with such an endeavor, good loca-tions and opportunities for a flipper might be a result that one could take advantage of.

Many other examples, government and private, exist across the country. Maybe in your area, a new state university campus or community college is being planned or built. Perhaps a man-ufacturer has experienced such success with its latest product line that it's planning to add additional manufacturing or assembly capacity in your town. As I've noted earlier, this expan-sion may be further fueled by some form of government eco-nomic assistance. Perhaps a continuing growth or reduction in the size of local population exists where you are, due, at least in part, to the climate where you are. Many "snow birds" from the northern states are moving to warmer climates, while many affected by recent calamities have left some parts of the South. Their destination may be your next place for a flip.

Investigate permits

At this point, it is not too early to consider looking at another government activity to help you decide whether to do a particu-lar flip or not. This activity is the area of entitlements. You must get the proper permits to do the construction of your project, and may even have to get a permit for the existing structure's demolition if a total gut is your plan. While there is not likely to be any local planning or building department that will give you blanket approval based solely on a discussion, it is always a good idea to go down to their offices and have a conversation or two with them about the general terms of what you'd like to do in their town or county. Typically, the conversation would run along the lines of you describing in at least some detail what you'd like to do, and have them go over with you what limits local applicable codes and ordinances may require of you. These could include such items as size of your project; design of the building; landscaping limits; special considerations in the case of hillside, lakeside, or riverbank work; setbacks; lot coverage limitations; height limitations; and the type and color of the material you plan to use for the outside of the structure when you are finishing that part of the project. You might even find that local ordinance limits what trees or plants you can uproot as part of your overall plan.

Here's a good example of why such information and conversation can be valuable. I recently handled the sale of a small century-old house in northern California. Due to the extremely small size of the lot, the most logical plan for the property—tear down the structure and build something completely new—was not possible. Local law would have precluded any attempt at such activity. In fact, had an owner completely torn down the existing house, he or she would have lost the "grandfathering" of the existing structure's size, and been allowed to build something only about 60 percent as large to replace it. (By "grandfathering," I mean that some things that would violate current code are allowed to remain because they pre-existed that code.

 Bright Idea

Be as detailed as possible about your plans with permitting authorities. Their information, ideas, and suggestions can provide you with useful information as you proceed. The more details you can provide, the better the quality of their response will be.

They have been "grandfathered" in.) Had this happened, the property's value would have been severely limited, and the chance for any profitability virtually eliminated. Clearly, a conversation with local authorities in such a situation is definitely in order and can help you avoid a complete disaster.

Maybe your project's in a hilly area. Local rules may limit how many changes in size or design you will be permitted to make, in the interests of safety to not only the ultimate occupants of your building, but also those farther down the hill from you. (In this situation, for example, a house sliding down a hill endangers both those living inside and anyone living farther down the hill.) Alternately, you may be permitted to build as large a structure as you'd like for your flip, but one of the requirements will be a large retaining wall and unusually thick foundations. These two requirements would not be required in a similar structure on flat land. The extra cost can destroy your budget, sometimes to the point that a decision *not* to flip there would be the wise one.

The point is, if you don't like what you are hearing from the local officials who will be required to approve your permits, you may decide to either change the scope and type of your flip, or move on entirely and look for something to flip in another locale. Yes, this is time consuming, but it is a great deal better to spend time and decide to not proceed with your venture than to not spend the time and get overwhelmed by the costs because you didn't do this bit of investigation.

Benefiting from disaster

Another factor regarding government action to consider in planning whether or not to undertake a specific flip is the response of local, state, or federal government to natural disasters. Often, there will be financial incentives provided for builders and/or property investors to become involved in the restoration or reconstruction of housing and other buildings in the wake of a natural disaster.

The best recent example of this is the fact that in certain parts of the Gulf Coast, an owner of rental residential property can take a "bonus" 50 percent of his or her purchase cost in depreciation in the first year of ownership. What does this have to do with your potential flip? Simple: It's an encouragement to likely buyers of property such as the type you may be considering flipping to do so. If the pool of potential buyers is increased in this manner, the chance of you successfully completing a project for a profit has just been enhanced. After all, more buyers means more competition for the product, and we all know what effect that has on the prices charged for the product.

Brain picking

Another source of information as you do your pre-project research is what I call "brain picking." Just as it sounds, this involves you picking the brains of others with experience for information to help you make the right decisions on your venture. The brains you will be picking in this case are those of others who've successfully done flips. Maybe they've done them in the past and are no longer doing them. There might be valuable information right there that could steer you away from an ill-conceived project. Maybe the folks you talk to have done flips before and continue to do so. They're experienced, knowledgeable, and continuing to succeed in their flipping activity. If the people with whom you speak have been doing flips for a long time, you can benefit from information of not only their successes, but also their failures. In the latter case, they may tell you something that they did—or failed to do—that would have made all the difference in the outcome and profitability of the particular project had they done just the opposite. This could be a valuable lesson.

The more of these veterans with whom you chat, the more information you'll gain. Admittedly, some of it will be of little value to you as it may be specifically anecdotal from a past project or projects. But there will definitely be information provided that you can use to help you succeed. It may be on the state of the local market, on tricks to make the work easier or more profitable, or some other bit of inside knowledge about how a particular municipality looks at certain types of construction activity. In this latter vein, you may even learn the identity of a particular building or planning officer who is easier to deal with on permits or, conversely, is "death" on almost

> **66** A good example of permit information that is valuable is the drainage requirements included in building codes for hillside sites. **99**
>
> —Tami, experienced flipper

anything new in a particular locale. Obviously, you'd attempt to hone in on or avoid that individual, whichever the case may be.

You might learn the name of a particular subcontractor who's expert at his type of work, and costs way below the going market rate. Maybe you'll discover a better, less expensive source for the granite counters you'd like to include in the kitchen and baths of your next flip. Perhaps you'll harvest a nugget about a source of top-quality salvaged trim or detail items that you can use in your restoration and flip of that Victorian cottage you've been looking at for your next venture. A client of mine who's done a couple of flips for profit, as well as major rehabs of properties for her own residence, has utilized just that type of salvaged items from the prior century for patio trim and an imposing handmade fireplace surround. Whatever you may learn, it is all useful to you as you proceed in your research.

Another potential benefit of this last bit of research is that you may find yourself talking with someone who would make a good partner for you on this or some future project. Perhaps your finances are going to be a bit tight for the project, or perhaps you feel that you'd like to have just a bit more expertise on a particular aspect than you yourself do. Assuming you feel comfortable with the individual whose brain you're busy picking, and the feeling appears to be mutual, you might consider bringing that person in on the project in one way or another.

A simple way of weighing all of these different sources is summarized in the following table. Ratings range from one to five stars, with five stars being the most important, and one star, the least important. You may wish to alter the ratings according to your own situation, but I think this provides a good tool in examining all factors.

Type of Information	Source	Importance Rating
Brain picking	Local flippers	★★★★★
How's the market?	Local Realtors	★★★★★
Demographics	Chamber of commerce, government	★★★★
Entitlements	Local planning or building department	★★★★
Economic considerations	Chamber of commerce, government	★★★
Infrastructure activity	Government	★★★
Government information	Chamber commerce, trade groups, Internet	★★
Natural disasters	Government	★

Just the facts

- Be thorough in your research; anything less can cost you a great deal of time, aggravation, and money.

- Government activity often foreshadows important changes in the local area that can boost or block conditions conducive to doing a flip.

- Major demographic changes are excellent indicators of the likely receptivity of a market to new real estate construction.

- Talk with building authorities about your project—they're the ones who will have the say on your obtaining necessary permits.
- *Always* talk with others who've flipped in your area; their personal experience can provide you excellent guidance in your project.

GET THE SCOOP ON...
Preparation is key ▪ An overview of the three
types of flips ▪ Deciding which type of flip is
best for you ▪ Flipping other types of properties

Deciding What Type of Flip to Do

Chapter 3

When you mention flipping to someone, the response you usually receive is a discussion on the total gutting and reconstruction of a house. In essence, folks usually think that to do a flip, you have to become the builder of an entirely new building. While that certainly is an option, it is far from the only one.

Which type of flip you decide to do will depend on a number of factors, including:

- Your budget
- The style and condition of the property you are considering for your flip
- The neighborhood where the property is situated
- Your experience in the process of flipping
- Market conditions in the area (both present and projected)
- Your own intentions regarding the particular property

The last of these, your intentions, can be as broad a subject area or as narrow as you may wish on a given project. While most folks do flips with the specific intent of selling them for profit at the completion of the construction, there may also be occasions where, due to market change since the start of construction, better opportunities, or personal financial reasons, you may consider retaining the property as a rental property, or, in the case of a multi-unit building, "codominiumizing" and selling the units one at a time.

The following items relate to a specific area and property you may be considering for your project. But there are many other factors that you must consider in making your decision. These are much broader than the items noted earlier, but equally important in assessing the big picture. As discussed in Chapter 2, these include:

- The general state of the economy
- Demographics in, and related to, the area
- The current rate of inflation
- How the employment picture is looking when you're going to be working on your flip

Personal concerns

Maybe this is your first attempt at a flip. You're understandably a bit nervous about the commitment you're making and the risks involved. After all, you've got to lay out a fairly good-sized chunk of cash (yours and the bank's) to buy the property to begin with. Then you will have to lay out additional sums to cover the cost of labor and materials involved in the makeover. Once you're finally finished, you'll have to pay a commission to the Realtor who's going to sell it for you, or you'll have to deal with the hassle of listing and selling it yourself (see Chapter 11 for information about selling a property). Remember, until it's sold, the interest meter is running. However, don't worry. If you prepare properly and analyze all aspects of the project, it should be

Bright Idea

As someone once said, "Experience is a great teacher." So, if you've done flips previously, you've already paid your tuition. It's going to be very helpful to use some of that education as you proceed with your next project.

successful—and perhaps become only the first of many successful ventures. I cannot overemphasize that preparation is at least as important as, if not more than, the actual work on the project.

On the other hand, perhaps you've done flips previously, and either you haven't been as fortunate in the outcome as you would have liked, or you're looking at expanding your horizons as to the type of flip to do next. Either way, there is no reason, given the proper preparation and analysis, that your current project shouldn't be as successful as, or even more successful than, your previous ones. You already know from experience at least some of the pitfalls that can occur, as well as the ways to either avoid them or at least minimize their effects.

The three types of flips

As I mentioned previously, flipping a property can mean a total redo of the structure from top to bottom. However, it does not have to be that involved. The choice is entirely yours! If you choose to do something less than a complete makeover and that's what you're comfortable with, fine. If this is your first experience with flipping, you may feel more comfortable starting at one of the easier levels before proceeding to more grandiose heights.

So, exactly what types of flips are there? For ease of discussion, I've divided potential projects into three general types. From the easiest and least expensive to the most difficult and most expensive, they are:

- Cosmetic
- Intermediate
- Total gut

I'll discuss each of these classifications in more detail in Chapters 10, 11, and 12, respectively. If you already think you know which type you're interested in, feel free to go straight to the chapter that deals with that particular form of flip.

The three types of flips I mention are, to some degree, so named because of the type of design and work you will be involved in as the project moves along toward completion and sale. Each is focused on a specific level of involvement determined by your goal, plans, and budget.

The cosmetic flip

A *cosmetic flip* is exactly what the name implies. The changes are largely cosmetic in nature—heavy reliance on paint and wallpaper, with maybe a bit of work on moldings and fixtures. Some structural work may be required to make the planned changes succeed, but the bulk of the work is focused strictly on increasing value, and thus your profit, by improving the surface appearance of the building, inside and out.

By "structural" changes, I do *not* mean replacing or expanding foundations, moving walls, or adding rooms or wings. The structural changes I refer to in this instance are far more basic and much simpler. They're limited to adding or enlarging doorways or windows and adding or changing skylights. This type of minor structural change can totally alter a potential buyer's impression of the finished product from satisfactory to "I've *got* to buy this house!" However, be aware that these minor structural alterations may have a higher cost attached to them than simpler items such as paint and paper. As with your materials cost for paint and wallpaper, this type of alteration is relatively minor.

In most cases, this type of change to a house is the least expensive, the quickest, and, often, the best opportunity for a higher percentage of profit.

This is because that old standard—the first impression—is the most important one in gaining a potential buyer's interest in purchasing your property. If the appearance of the property causes the potential buyer to perceive increased value, he or she will be more likely to pay you more money for your efforts. Remember, in today's world, especially in real estate, perception *is* reality.

> **❝**It's important to remember that the more expensive the project is, the more real cash profit you receive from a certain percentage profit gain—25 percent of a $300,000 investment is more than 25 percent of a $200,000 flip.**❞**
>
> —Robert, experienced flipper

If you're doing a cosmetic flip, you need to be absolutely certain that the basic structure of the building is sound. There is nothing worse than planning and budgeting for a relatively low-cost project only to find out that the foundation or some other major component of the property is shot and needs replacing—something that is only possible with a major expenditure of your money. If you fail to look for these kinds of problems early, you may end up eliminating the bulk of your projected profit. In Chapter 7, I'll discuss how inspections can help you avoid this profit-killer.

The idea of improving a potential buyer's perception of the property with a minimum of effort and expense should also include some upgrades to the landscaping. Curb appeal—the emotional impact on buyers when they first arrive at the curb—can *never* be overstated as to its importance in getting your property sold. You don't need to spend thousands on landscaping in a cosmetic job. You can succeed with as little as the addition of an array of new flowers or shrubbery, or, if the lawn looks ratty, the installation of new sod. This is important, because even if you've redone the interior to the nines, many people won't even stop the car to go inside a house if the outside looks terrible. A few hundred dollars in landscaping can add thousands to your sales price. It's all about the first impression the house creates.

The intermediate flip

The *intermediate flip* involves a higher level of work than the cosmetic flip. In additional to visual improvements such as painting and landscaping, you do major construction work in some part or parts of the home—a new kitchen and master bath, for example. You might even add a wing or second story and then leave almost everything else for cosmetics, but still limit this activity to a level well short of a total gut. Clearly, the extent of the structural changes or additions increases the amount of time, effort, and money involved, and gets you closer to a total gut. But, as long as you're retaining most of the original structure, it's considered an intermediate flip.

Along with the increased amount of time, material, and money involved with an intermediate flip, there are a number of other items that need your full attention. As you'll be doing some construction, you'll need the services of an architect to draw plans for whatever construction work is involved.

Depending on the site of the house, you may also find it necessary to engage other professionals such as drainage experts, soil engineers, or structural engineers.

For example, an intermediate flip on flat stable land probably only needs consultation with a structural engineer regarding any expansion or strengthening of the foundation, while doing the same intermediate flip on or adjacent to a hillside may also require that individual's expertise in designing special retaining walls to ensure that the house remains on the hill where you found it and does not slide down the hill after the first heavy rain. Also, features of this nature mean hiring additional contractors who specialize in this type of work.

As always, one thing leads to another. If your intermediate flip requires these extra features, you'll very likely have to get additional permits, which, as with the advice of the professionals already referred to, will increase the overall cost.

 Moneysaver

Depending on the extent of the changes, consider using a home CAD system such as 3-D-Home Architect.

The total gut

A *total gut* is just that—the total gutting or even the tearing down and rebuilding of the property. There are differing levels of this as well. The easiest, in some cases, involves leaving the four walls standing and totally tearing out and rebuilding everything inside. The opposite extreme involves tearing the home down to the bare ground and starting fresh, just as if there never had been a house on the site before you purchased it. Which approach you choose depends on your pre-project preparation, budget, and analysis.

The additional items you need to consider for a total gut are much of the same type as for an intermediate flip, but because of the larger size of the project, there are many more of them.

Which type of flip is right for you?

This is an important decision to make—possibly the most important one of all, as it determines the amount of time, money, materials, and risk you'll have to be dealing with on your flip. Possibly the best thing to help you make this decision is to ask yourself a series of questions. These questions, and the answers you come up with to them, may not by themselves make your final determination, but they will go a long way to helping you reach your decision. This list is only a sampling, but a very good start, and your own question list will be as varied as the projects you consider:

- How much time do I want to spend on this project?
- What is the budget for each type?
- What type flip is the market currently favoring?
- What do the demographics favor?
- What's the availability of the contractors/professionals I'll need for each type of flip?
- How much experience do I have in each flip type?

Carefully analyze all items affecting your choice. More time spent at this point can save you a great deal of aggravation and expense later on, no matter which flip format you choose.

Chapters 10, 11, and 12 examine the different types of flips in greater detail, along with discussing a number of choices that you can make in developing your unique project. But first, I want to make a very important point: *No one type of flip is more correct or proper than any other.* Perhaps one individual would prefer to do a cosmetic flip on a small country cottage, while another has the time, energy, experience, personnel, and funding to undertake the total gutting and reconstruction of a huge mansion. Some people prefer to do *only* cosmetics, while others put the bulk of their energy and funds into reworking one specific part of the house, for the most part just cosmetically improving the balance. These folks may do this over and over and over again on property after property. If you find a formula that you are comfortable with and good at, there's no reason not to stick with it. Do what you want to do and what makes you comfortable. After careful consultation, planning, and budgeting, go for it!

Flipping other properties

There are many different types of flips that can be undertaken. Flips are not by any means limited to residential properties. Flips are commonly undertaken with an entire spectrum of property, including:

- Apartment houses or hotels, often converted to condominiums
- Office buildings
- Mixed-use properties that may include a number of varied types of space within their walls

However, for the purposes of this book, I'll be concentrating mainly on the traditional single-family detached house.

Just the facts

- Pick a type of flip you're comfortable with—then go with it!
- As the value of your project grows, so does the profit in actual dollars received as a percentage of your investment.
- Curb appeal is important—it makes prospective buyers want to get into the house to see your work.
- Choose your type of flip carefully; as the size and cost increase, so do the risks—and hopefully, the profit.

GET THE SCOOP ON...
Have an honest conversation with yourself ▪
Checking in with others ▪ A final review of
government activity ▪ Making the decision:
flip or quit?

Conversations: Moving Forward

Chapter 4

Now is the time to start talking with yourself about your proposed flip, and with much more intensity. You have already carefully considered the idea of even doing any kind of flip, and, as I suggested in Chapter 3, have asked yourself detailed questions to help determine exactly what kind of flip you'll undertake. Up to this point, the idea of doing a flip has been just that—an idea. However, now the discussion takes on much more gravity.

It's very much like a military campaign. The generals think about all of the things that they have to do to prepare to go into battle at a particular time and place before ever firing the first shot. When the final stages of their planning occur, they must carefully review everything involved before going ahead or deciding to scrub the battle plan altogether. It's the same here.

A conversation with yourself

Start your "conversation" with a thorough review of why you even want to do a flip. Closely examine the projected profits and ROI you think you can expect from your project, as well as your analysis of the ROI for this type of investment as opposed to others on the market. While you're at it, also review your analysis of the comparative risks for your project versus the risks inherent in other types of investments. At this point in your review, also look carefully and *honestly* at your appetite for the risk that your flip will carry, as opposed to the level of risk in competing investments. I emphasize the factor of honesty here because there are times when emotion will overcome good judgment, and you'll lie to yourself, unintentionally, about the qualities of your goal, when you should perhaps consider them with a bit more reservation.

Has your enthusiasm for doing the flip waned or is it still high? What effect will doing the flip have on those close to you (spouse/significant other and family)? It may seem silly to think of these things when considering a flip, but once you're in the middle of the project and something goes even slightly sideways, you'd be amazed how much tension that can place on personal life and relationships.

Also, you need to maintain balance in your daily life. If you normally take a certain amount of time daily or weekly to run, bike, pursue a hobby, or whatever, that should not be sacrificed in the name of the flip. You'll find you need that "normal" time as a balance. It'll also help you maintain your sense of humor and sanity if and when something fails to go the way you've planned.

 Bright Idea

You don't necessarily have to limit the participants in the conversation to just yourself. If you have someone whose judgment and business acumen you trust, there's no reason not to discuss the potential flip with that person.

Watch Out!

Carefully review *all* details on entitlements. Your discussions may reveal issues that will make profitability impossible.

Review the state of the real estate market, and carefully evaluate the projected state of that same market at the time when you expect to be putting your finished product on the market. In this part of your conversation, re-examine exactly what forces are driving the property market, and what forces are expected to be moving the market at your completion date. Are they the same, or are new factors expected to emerge that may make or break the profitable sale of your finished flip?

Re-examine what you've learned about the ease or difficulty of obtaining your entitlements. The permitting process can make or break any part of your project just by the degree of difficulty and time it takes to obtain the necessary permits. Extra time at this juncture will mean more money spent on interest and on assistance from your professional team (architects, engineers, attorney, and CPA).

Expanding the conversation

If you're working with a Realtor, you may need to call him or her again. What market information are you receiving from this quarter that will show with what degree of ease or difficulty your project will sell? Has the market dramatically changed since you first spoke to your agent? If so, has it improved or deteriorated in that time? If it hasn't yet changed, are there indications that it is likely to do so during the period that you will be engaged in finishing your project? Such changes may dictate that you either go forward, quit, or possibly alter the overall scope of your project. You may decide to expand it, or cut it back, say, from an intermediate to a cosmetic flip. (See Chapter 3 for an overview of the three types of flips.)

Moneysaver

Your bank and the U.S. Department of Commerce often have economic projections that can indicate the direction of the economy—and, by inference,
its effects on your project.

If one of the items that originally dictated a type of flip has
changed, should your flip type change—or go forward at all? Is
the size of that new plant going to be larger or smaller than originally envisioned? Has the marketplace for its products improved
or deteriorated?

Talk with your sources of funding. If you have equity partners, make sure that they're still fully on board with the flip. Has
anything in their personal financial lives changed that may limit
their financial participation? Perhaps there has been a business
loss, severe illness with only partial insurance coverage, or
change in family status that will impact their ability to be your
partner. A partner to a flip may drop out due to a divorce settlement or other major life change.

Next, a final consultation with your lenders is in order. Just
make certain that money for your project is still available and at
a reasonable price. Even if your credit rating is still good, it is
very possible that an oncoming adverse market in real estate or
rebalancing of the lender's loan portfolio may preclude their
lending as much money to you, or even making any loan at all.

Your conversation with the bank should review the current
interest rates. Have they remained where they were when you
got your initial approval, or are they higher or lower? Are there
any new fees that the lender has put on loan programs that perhaps didn't exist when you last spoke with the lender? We'll
touch on this area again in Chapter 5 as part of the setting of
your budget, and examine it in great detail in Chapter 8 where
we discuss financing in depth.

Be aware that there is a lot of confusion between "pre-qualification" and "pre-approval":

- *Pre-qualification* means that you have a letter, at best, from your finance source saying that you appear to be qualified for financing at some time in the near future, subject to that lender doing a full analysis and underwriting of the loan request. It could also add, "This paper is worth about the value of the paper—no more," but it won't. The point is, the lender thinks reasonably well of your creditworthiness after probably a five-minute conversation, but isn't committing any money to you yet. If your lender has pre-qualified you, you don't have final approval for your financing.

- *Pre-approval* means that your financing request has undergone full analysis and underwriting and been approved, usually subject only to the lender seeing an appraisal and preliminary title report.

One last check of government activity

Another area in which to do one final review is government activity. This includes the government's reactions to "acts of God." Has there been any activity on the part of any government—federal, state, county, or local—that could have an effect on the success of your planned flip? Have new taxes been written into law, or the existing ones increased? Have taxes been reduced?

Frequently, governments will take some form of economic action to encourage development of a certain locale, either to encourage population growth in an area or to strengthen the local economic base there. Check one last time with the relevant government authorities to see if your flip qualifies for any type of incentive that exists or is being planned.

In the case of natural disasters or "acts of God," there are often a variety of economic incentives or tax benefits offered to real estate developers who help in the reconstruction of the devastated area. While such incentives usually focus on large-scale new development, it doesn't hurt to check with the appropriate authority to see if your flip qualifies.

A good recent example of this is in the Baton Rouge, Louisiana, area. As a direct result of the devastation from Hurricane Katrina in 2005, many people fled inland from New Orleans to Baton Rouge, severely straining that area's local housing. In an effort to encourage investment in rental residential property in Baton Rouge, the federal government provided a bonus 50 percent depreciation of purchase price on such property. Would a flip in the area qualify? Conversely, would it make sense to acquire Katrina-damaged property in New Orleans and try a flip there? This is a question that you would put to the appropriate authorities and your CPA. If so, it could increase the profitability of your project.

Make the decision

You've planned carefully. You've reviewed all of the factors that could affect your proposed project. It's decision time! Do you proceed with your flip, put it off until a better time, or quit altogether?

You may decide, for whatever reason, that the wisest choice at this time is to quit. There's no shame in that. If you decide after careful consideration that you can do your flip, but only at a loss or with marginal ROI, then stopping before you spend any more time or money is a very wise decision. If the timing's bad at the present time, you may wish to reconsider next year, or if a local new development, private or government, is announced at some future time.

Perhaps interest rates have gone up to an unacceptable level. You may decide to wait until they either flatten or drop a bit.

On the other hand, you may weigh all the facts and say, "Let's go!" In that case, it's time to begin the hard work—doing your flip. But don't worry—it'll be fun, and, if you've planned correctly, profitable.

Just the facts

- Do some unemotional, honest soul searching about the financial and personal aspects of your proposed flip.

- Seek out and seriously consider the wisdom of others.

- When checking government activity, make certain you cover all government levels—local, state, and federal.

- Make your final decision *only* after you've thoroughly investigated everything and reviewed the information you've obtained.

GET THE SCOOP ON...
Budget considerations ▪ Acquisition, soft, and
hard costs ▪ Factoring in unexpected costs ▪ Tax
implications ▪ Making a profit

Setting Your Budget

Chapter 5

This part of a flipping project is totally paper and brainpower. You'll do no on-site work at all, with two exceptions.

First, you'll probably spend time looking at potential properties that your Realtor, if you're using one, finds for your consideration as purchases. For those of you not using a Realtor, for whatever reason, you'll still spend a fair amount of time looking at properties via newspaper ads, open houses, the Internet, and "For Sale" signs hung by owners.

Second, you'll spend time walking the property immediately after you've had your offer accepted by the seller as you start to physically lay out your project in your head as well as on sketch paper.

With these exceptions, however, the bulk of your work here will be with pencil, paper, calculator, and computer. Oh, yes—and don't forget the telephone.

Budgeting for your project

Chances are you already have some idea of what the maximum is that you want to spend on the project. You probably have an idea of what you believe you can afford. Otherwise, you probably wouldn't have gotten even to this early stage in the process. However, there is still work to do even here.

You may find after a chat with your lender, bank, or mortgage broker that you can afford to spend *more* than you originally thought. For example, you may have thought that all you could afford was a total expenditure—your capital and the bank's loan together—of $300,000. After you sit down with your mortgage broker, you discover that you can actually afford a total expenditure of $400,000. If you're like most people at this stage, you have a couple of different reactions. Your initial reaction is likely to be, "Wow! That's great! I'm even better off than I suspected!" But upon further consideration, you may feel the larger amount is more than you want to spend or feel comfortable spending. I often see this with buyers, regardless of whether they're buying their first home, a large office building, or a property to flip.

That's fine. There's no shame in not spending every last dime on a purchase just because your lender assures you that you can afford to do so. Remember—it's *your* project. If you planned to spend only a total of $300,000 on your project, you feel comfortable only up to that level, and you know from initial research that such an amount will enable you to complete your project, then stay with that amount. As you'll see when you prepare your formal budget for the project, you'll have some extra items added in that could provide for slight increases beyond the overall amount from your planned level.

As you'll see later in this chapter, one area that could lead to a slight increase in your overall expenditures is the contingency expense account. Another is the sudden decision to increase

 Moneysaver

There are a large number of software programs that can assist you in financial planning, timeline, and design work for your project.

Watch Out!

Don't let yourself go overboard financially just because you discover you can afford more on paper than you feel comfortable spending.

expenditures on a part of the flip because of a particular change in conditions or because an unexpected opportunity arises during the project. However, start with a particular target that you do not want to exceed. Then do all your planning based on that figure.

Cost considerations

Costs arise in any type of real estate development project, and a flip is one of them. Costs are usually divided into three types: acquisition costs, soft costs, and hard costs. Let's take a closer look at each.

Acquisition costs

Put simply, your *acquisition cost* is the actual price you pay to buy the house you intend to flip. It may seem obvious, but this amount should be included in any flip budget, because it likely is the largest single cost of the entire enterprise.

As with your overall budget, you must decide what is the maximum you're willing to pay to acquire the property. Part of this decision will be based on the type of flip you plan on doing (see Chapter 3). Obviously, if you're doing a cosmetic flip, you'll likely be buying a home that is already in fairly good structural condition. Therefore, you'll pay a bit more than you would for a property that has structural issues, or one to which you'll be making major structural changes or additions, such as you'd find in either an intermediate flip or a total gut job. Similarly, if you're planning on a total gut, you'll likely be looking for a structure that is in such poor condition, or so out of date, that the only thing to do is to tear it down and start from the ground up, or close to it. In such a case, you'd be paying much less for a property.

There are sometimes exceptions to this if, for example, the proposed property is in an area of high prices and skyrocketing market values with lots of competition for everything that hits the market. In such a case, you may well pay top dollar for the property. A case in point: Just a few weeks before I wrote this section, a small three-bedroom property (divided into two units) in a popular area in northern California, on a lot slightly over a quarter acre in size, was priced at just over $1 million, but received ten offers and sold for over $1.2 million—all for a home that's to be torn down and replaced by a new one that will likely sell for more than $3 million.

Exactly what you plan to do to change the property to complete the flip may well depend at least in part on how much the acquisition costs you. If you've got only a certain amount of money to use in the whole budget, every dollar you expend acquiring the house is one dollar less that you have to do the work that will be necessary to remake it and prepare it for resale. Also, it will directly affect your profit at the conclusion of the flip.

Inspections

Under the category of acquisition costs, there are two other areas of expense. The first is inspections and due diligence. You'll want to know as much as possible about the physical condition of the property before you take title. A thorough inspection may reveal previously unknown defects that result in you successfully negotiating a price reduction from the seller. You'll do as many inspections as you feel are necessary, often with your Realtor's advice. Normally, this will be at least a pest or termite inspection and a contractor's home inspection. If something out of the ordinary turns up in these inspections—say, issues with the foundation or the roof—you may also have someone inspect the items in question. If the home sits in a topographically unusual or dangerous area, you may want to have additional inspections for such things as retaining walls, soils, and drainage.

Watch Out!

Don't assume that if you overspend to buy the house, you'll "make it up in the end" with a higher sales price. If you're in a rapidly appreciating market, you *might* get away with just adding to the selling price of your finished product, but this is not something to blithely take for granted.

A lot of this will depend on your own experience in the actual construction. If you've done many properties previously, you may not put as much weight on independent inspections, relying instead on your own expertise. But whatever inspections you do will carry a cost, ranging anywhere from several hundred to several thousand dollars.

Closing costs

The remaining acquisition cost is closing costs. These include such items as escrow fees, title insurance, recording costs, loan points, and notary fees, as well as various other fees that may be typical in your particular locale. A good general rule for estimating closing costs is about 3 percent of your purchase price.

Soft costs

Soft costs are the expenses you must pay to the professionals who help you develop your flip from an idea to an identifiable tangible product. For example, fees paid to the following types of professionals would fall under soft costs:

- Attorneys
- Architects and engineers
- Accountants
- Lenders
- Insurers
- Permits

Soft costs get their name because they are just that: soft. They are not incurred to purchase objects that you can lay your hands on, such as lumber or sheetrock, but they are just as real, and can have as much of an effect on your project as the costs incurred for such items.

Some soft costs are set by local government agencies and bear little, if any, relationship to the cost of your project. Instead, these costs depend more on the local governing authority's budgetary needs or use of the fees to enforce certain ordinances or policies. Some soft costs are payable as a percentage of the overall budget, while others are done on a time-based fee for work performed. Still others are paid based on the overall price for which you ultimately sell your completed project.

However, soft costs are very real, and they do come out of your pocket just as certainly as the actual construction costs will. You will pay most, though not all, of these costs before you ever drive a single nail or tear out a single wall. Some will be paid, at least in part, before you even obtain your permits (yet another type of soft costs).

Industry sources and lenders generally agree that the effects of the passage of time on your costs are another factor you must consider. As a general rule, you can count on it costing you about 1.5 percent of the property's original value each month that you own it. This is the best example of the adage "Time is money" that I know of, and definitely one to remember when planning the project timeline.

You can minimize this factor to some extent if you plan to have as much work done simultaneously on the property as possible. For example, you could have the electrical work, tiling, and plumbing handled at the same time, but by different contractors, rather than consecutively. Thus, you've saved some

Moneysaver

You can reduce project time by carefully planning your materials delivery and labor schedules well in advance. Every month you save is roughly 1.5 percent of the project's value.

time in getting your project completed. If the original cost of your property was $200,000, and you cut off a month in construction time by doing this, you save roughly $3,000. That goes straight to the bottom line—your profits. Additionally, well-planned delivery of materials to the site can save time and money. There's nothing worse than having workers ready on site and no material for them to use due to delays or inadequately planned delivery times.

Attorneys

The first place you may want to spend money is at your attorney's. If you don't already have an attorney, get one!

Why should you have an attorney? After all, you're doing a real estate project, not a corporate takeover or defending yourself in court. The reason is simple: It is to provide you with as much legal protection as possible as you proceed with the flip. Should something go south during the project, it would be much better for you if all your assets were not exposed to potential liability. It would be far better if only the assets connected to the project had possible legal exposure.

An attorney can attempt to provide you with this type of protection. Very likely, he or she will recommend that you form a limited liability corporation (LLC) for this purpose. The LLC becomes the owner and developer of the flip, as opposed to you personally. In actual practice, there may be no difference once the hard work gets underway. However, in terms of liability, there can be a world of difference. If events turn against you, the relatively few dollars you spend here may save you a great deal more at the end of the day.

How do you choose an attorney? You can do a number of things. Ask your friends, business associates, or others you know who do flips for their recommendations. A referral based on good, solid experience can be invaluable. This type of referral can also come from your accountant. Another method is to contact the local bar association. Most have some form of attorney referral service based on the type of legal issues you have to address. This type of referral service from the bar association is also usually free.

Get a few recommendations and then do as you would when hiring anyone: Interview that person. Perhaps the attorney who's regarded as the "dean" of the practice just doesn't mesh well with your personality or approach. Maybe the next lawyer on the referral list is a better fit for you.

During your interviews with attorneys, proceed as you would in any interview. Tell the lawyer in some detail about your plans and desires and see what methods he or she uses to approach these subjects. Ask if the attorney has any new ideas on the subject or is on top of the latest developments in the legal area on this particular subject. Ask what degree of experience on the subject that attorney has. You don't necessarily need to have an attorney who's handled over 10,000 flips or the limited liability corporations used to protect the flippers, but, on the other hand, you don't want to be the individual's "maiden flip" LLC. Another item you'll want to know is the attorney's fee for such work. Does she have a flat fee for doing an LLC, or does she charge by the hour for the job?

If the attorney to whom you're talking is a partner in a firm as opposed to a sole practitioner or one of a group of two or three attorneys, ask if he or she will be doing the work for you, or if an associate fresh out of law school will. If it's the latter, you'll want to know how the fee structure varies based on how much of the work is the associate's and how much is the partner's.

Another item you'll want to discuss is the availability of the attorney. Perhaps this firm has so much work it cannot really do justice to another new client at the present time. Also, it may be able to take on a client, but not be as available as your needs may require, based on your own experience in the realm of flipping. It's better to find out now rather than when an emergency arises requiring immediate consultation with counsel.

Go through this process with as many attorneys as you feel necessary, but don't spend so much time doing it that you lose track of everything else. You'll probably find the right attorney for your needs after you've spoken to three or four. Remember—there's still your project to get working on.

Once you've chosen your attorney, have an LLC created for the project. Some flippers use one LLC for all their flips. Others have a new one created for each project. I prefer the latter, but check with your attorney. After all, you hired this person, in part, for his or her legal advice.

In addition to the attorney's fee for the work, you'll likely pay a fee to have the corporation registered or recorded in accordance with local law. You may also wish to spend a few dollars for stationery and business cards for the LLC if you think you'll need them going forward.

Architects and engineers

Next come the design costs. You can't calculate actual work and the cost for it until you actually buy the property you're going to flip, especially if you're going to do anything beyond the most basic of cosmetic flips. This is because the architect and engineer cannot possibly make any specific design recommendations or plans without knowing the location and size of the lot, its geographical details, and the local ordinances of the town where the house will be built. However, they can tell you what their fee structures are, and whether they're based on the job involved, the overall project cost, or a per-hour fee.

Some architects work on a fee based on a percentage of the overall project budget, often 10 to 15 percent of the budget exclusive of their fee. Others will discuss your project with you

---

 Moneysaver

You won't likely need an architect for a cosmetic flip. There's no structural work to do. You *may* need one for an intermediate flip, but only if you're adding on a wing or doing some similar redesign that requires major structural work. Due to the volume of structural work involved, you *will* use an architect for a total gut. There, you'll be totally redesigning the house.

in some detail, and quote a specific fee for the work. Still others will quote an hourly fee, and tell you that they don't expect it to take more than a certain amount of time to do the work.

Engineering services are a different design element. Usually, this type of work is contracted for in conjunction with the architect, and sometimes may even be engaged in your behalf by the architect and billed as part of his overall fee. Engineering expertise may be necessitated by something as normal as the construction plans for the foundation or something as unique and property specific as a large retaining wall on a hillside or analysis of soils prior to construction to ensure that your project won't collapse just as you're driving the final nail. The engineer may be engaged to ensure the dimensions and details of the foundation, particularly in structures involving more than a single story. Usually, the costs of the engineer are billed on an hourly basis, sometimes with an estimated maximum at the bottom of the projected cost. As with the architect, the less structural work or alterations your project will involve, the lower the cost of the engineer is likely to be.

Accountants

Depending on how formal you plan to be in your finance-related activity on the flip, your accountant may maintain running accounts, including accounts payable, banking accounts, and expenditures, throughout the life of the project.

Equally important, he or she may also handle your tax liabilities and deductions arising from the project. Assuming you realize a profit at the end of the day, you will likely have a tax liability to address. How that is handled, to your best advantage, is something your accountant will discuss in great detail with you. Are you eligible for lower capital gains rates, or must you pay regular income tax rates on your profits? If you decide that you want to do another flip, or invest your profits in income property, can you defer the tax liability through a 1031 Exchange? We will deal with all aspects of accounting issues such as these in greater depth in Chapter 17.

Lenders

Another expense to consider as part of your soft costs is interest. Unless you're planning to use only your own cash, or yours and that of any partners you have, you'll be financing your acquisition of the property and the following work with money borrowed from a lending source. Whether it's a bank, a credit union, an insurance company, or a friend is irrelevant. Whatever your source of funding, interest will be charged on the loan for the life of the loan. Ask various lenders what their cost of funding is for the type of loan you'll receive from them. There may be two separate loans, one to acquire the house, and a second to do the work; or there may be only one, the original acquisition loan folding into a construction loan to finish the project.

The interest charged may be payable on a regular schedule as specified in the loan agreement, perhaps monthly or quarterly. It may just be an expense that you're expected to come up with from your own resources. However, in many cases, loans from institutional lenders have an increased principal amount to include the item known as an interest reserve. This additional amount of money added to your requested loan amount is there strictly to make lenders feel sure they'll get their interest payments on time. In essence, banks require you to borrow more money than you'd originally intended so that they get paid on time during the construction period when you presumably have no income from the subject property.

Insurers

There are a number of different types of insurance to consider over the life of your project, some only at different phases of the project and others throughout the period that you legally own the property.

The most common of these types of insurance is what is referred to as casualty insurance. As the name suggests, it covers you in the event you (or your flip) suffer some form of casualty loss. It might be a physical injury to a worker or visitor to the location of your flip. It also includes any physical damage to the

structure at any time during your ownership, as well as any physical damage or loss of your materials, tools, or equipment on the
site.

Suppose you have just finished framing up the structure of a
new room you are adding in an intermediate flip and a short
circuit causes a fire, burning down not only your new work, but
most of the rest of the house as well.

In another instance, about two months after you've acquired
the house you're going to flip, the tenant you've allowed to
remain in the house while you go through the permitting
process gets careless around the fireplace and causes a fire that
causes substantial damage to the living room of what you were
planning to do only a cosmetic flip on.

Perhaps you have just finished most of the construction on a
total gut and are just weeks from having your Realtor place it on
the market. Unfortunately, the locale of your flip is hit with a
week's worth of torrential rains and the nearby streams overflow
their banks, flooding the neighborhood—including your
almost-finished house.

I could continue in this vein, but you probably get the picture.
All of the above have happened to property owners, often during
flips, and will always continue to be a consideration during the
process of flipping. There are other potential casualty losses you
could face, including earthquake, landslide, hail, or vandalism.

You might also have a visitor to the building trip and fall, suf-
fering some injury or other. It could be your architect, your
Realtor, or a curious neighbor not paying attention to the "Do
Not Trespass—Construction Zone" warning signs. A limb from
that magnificent century-old oak in the front yard could break
off and crush a passing car. All of these incidents are also types
of casualty losses you could suffer. It is far better to let someone
else—an insurance company—pay for the resulting damage or
fight the lawsuit than to have to do so yourself.

Budget for the premiums and buy the insurance policy or
policies necessary for your coverage. I say "policies" because some
things are *not* covered by a basic property casualty insurance

Bright Idea

If you live in an area that is seismically active (most of the West Coast, Alaska, Hawaii, and the area between Memphis and St. Louis), you should seriously consider earthquake insurance. Damage from earthquakes is not covered by the normal casualty policy. Deductibles are larger and this type of coverage is very expensive, but far less so than the cost of replacing all or most of your building.

policy. For example, flood damage is not covered. For flood damage, you need a flood insurance policy. In some cases, landslide damage is not covered by the typical casualty policy. It depends on whether the slide is considered to be caused by movement of land or by water starting the slide.

Two types of non-casualty insurance you should consider purchasing are completion bonds and workman's compensation insurance. The first is something that you normally wouldn't worry about unless your project had unusually risky circumstances that could threaten the likelihood of it being completed. Usually, it comes into play on larger projects, and even then, most likely as a condition of the bank's financing of the project. Workman's compensation, often referred to as workman's comp, covers a worker injured on the job who cannot work for a given period, thus threatening his or her income. If you engage a contractor or subcontractors for your work, it is likely that they will already have this coverage for their workers. Ask these contractors when you engage them for the job. Don't just take their word for it. Have them show you evidence of a current policy for this. If they do not have it, you may want to give serious consideration to purchasing it. Again, it would be a great deal cheaper to have to pay the premiums for a few months than to have to compensate one or more workers injured by some accident on your project.

Other soft costs

There are a couple of additional soft cost items to include in your budget. The first is what I call non-income taxes. The most common of this type of tax is property tax. One of the best sources of revenue for all local governments, its existence is almost universal in one form or another. While the method of its calculation may differ greatly from one jurisdiction to another, its existence is undeniable. Basically, it is a tax paid at least annually that is charged on some form of valuation of the real property being taxed. Like it or not, this is an item you'll have to pay, and the longer you own the property in question, the larger the total amount of tax charged will be.

Another form of tax charged in some locales is a transfer tax. It is usually calculated on the sale price of the property and paid by the seller. This means that when you complete your flip and put it on the market, if you're in one of the areas that charges this type of tax, you'll pay a percentage of your sale price to the local government as tax on the sale. In California, for example, this tax is statewide, and is calculated at $1.10 for every thousand dollars of sale price. This means that if you sell your flip for $500,000 in California, you'll pay $550 to the government in transfer tax.

The final soft cost item that must be included in your budget is the commission you'll pay your Realtor, should you use one, to sell your finished flip. Obviously this amount varies from area to area and agent to agent. Also, with the advent of so-called "discount" brokers, in some areas there is a great deal of downward pressure on commissions. A word to the wise here— and this also applies to trying to sell the flipped house by yourself to save a commission—you usually get what you pay for, even in real estate brokerage and marketing. As a good friend

Bright Idea

When assembling your budget, check with local authorities as well as your Realtor, if you're using one, to see if there are any other locally unique forms of taxes that will affect your project, and, if so, make sure you include them in your budget.

and excellent agent put it, "You don't get Nordstrom's quality shopping at Wal-Mart." Figure on paying 5 to 7 percent as a commission. Possibly, if you're using the same agent over and over to buy and sell, you may get some break on the commission based on the continuity and volume of business you do with him or her, but, again, that's something to work out directly with your own agent.

> **❝** Although one does not have to use a Realtor, as a buyer, there's virtually no reason not to, and huge benefits in using one. **❞**
>
> —Robert, experienced flipper

You may decide you can handle the flip without a Realtor. If you have the knowledge of the market and how to sell a property, there is no reason to insist you use a Realtor. If you have the experience in what's involved in successfully marketing a property, you can do what's referred to as a FSBO (For Sale By Owner) and not engage a Realtor (see Chapter 16 for more on the FSBO). You will save the commission I mentioned but will have to absorb a portion of that amount in your marketing expenses—flyers, print ads, and Internet expenses, to name a few. It's worth some consideration.

Hard costs

Hard costs are, as the term suggests, the expenses you incur in the actual work on the project. They involve tangible, physical material and labor that can be visibly followed as you proceed with the project's development. As you budget for these costs, you likely will not account for every last nail and screw or piece of tile. However, you'll carefully cost out the expenses necessary in obtaining all the materials you plan to use in your project, regardless of what type of flip you envision. If, for example, you're planning on a cosmetic flip, you'll carefully measure the space inside the house to be certain that you account for the necessary amount of paint, whether you're doing the work yourself or retaining the services of a painting contractor.

If your project's a more involved one—an intermediate flip or a total gut—you and your contractor will carefully review the existing space and the living area to account for pricing and ordering all the various items that will go into the property, including:

- Tile or stone for counters in the kitchen and/or bath(s)

- Lumber or shingles for siding

- Roofing materials

- Fixtures and pipes for not only the bathrooms and kitchen, but also additional outlets in the garage, basement, den, patio, and so on

Similar concerns will have to be met and dealt with in budgeting your costs for the electrical system in the house. Will the existing panel be enough for what you have planned, or will it need to be replaced with a larger one?

Then you consider glass. What type of windows, both style and amount of glass per window, are you going to use? In most areas today, double-paned windows have become fairly common. Although they are more expensive than single-paned windows, double-paned windows lead to great savings in the heating and cooling of a home, as the extra pane of glass adds insulating capacity. In fact, in some areas of the country, new construction is required by code to include nothing less than double-pane construction. Carrying this a bit further, triple-paned windows also exist, mostly for sections of the country that regularly experience extreme cold. Again, these windows are more expensive, but the extra layer of glass helps greatly in insulating the property while limiting the increased amounts of fuel necessary to keep the inside of the house at a comfortable temperature when outside temperatures drop.

Consider what effect different types of designs will have on the cost of a particular part of your project. For instance, will you add French doors to the yard or patio, or merely have the architect plan for a sliding glass door? The latter is usually cheaper, and, depending on the overall scope of your project and the price point and expected design details for properties in your market, may be the more common or desirable.

Labor expense

The cost of labor can be established in two ways. If you hire a general contractor and use his or her subcontractors for the various separate tasks such as electrical, plumbing, and roofing, you can get a contract for the entire job, or as much as the contractor includes in the overall bid, that will have an overall price that you can factor into your budget.

Alternatively, you may choose to contract with one contractor for the construction and hire different contractors for each individual portion of the work, such as tile and stone work, painting, and cabinetry. Whichever way you decide to proceed, you will have a definite cost for the necessary labor that you can factor into your budget.

Planning for the unexpected

"Well," you're probably saying, "I guess my budget's ready to proceed." In fact, it *almost* is. There is one other item to consider. There is probably no other single area where Murphy's Law crops up so frequently as construction. If you're not familiar with it, Murphy's Law is the unwritten rule that says, "If something can possibly go wrong, it will." It's an unfortunate fact of life.

Something totally unexpected happens to mess up your plans. It rains a month longer than normal in your territory and the painting of the house is delayed, causing you to miss a month of the spring selling market. A short circuit in the home's old wiring causes a fire that severely damages two rooms and you'd only planned on a cosmetic flip. A trucking strike causes delivery of all of your double-paned windows to be delayed two months.

Any of these things can happen, and most have at one time or another, as well as dozens of others too numerous to recount here. The point is, they will cause you less financial pain if you provide some advance planning for the eventuality in your budget.

You do this by adding a "contingency" expense. Generally, the contingency expense is calculated as 10 percent of the total construction budget. So, if your overall construction budget is $75,000, the contingency expense you will add to the budget is $7,500.

> 66 I always use 20 percent contingency. The extra is to make up for the "wishful thinking" factor. 99
>
> —Robert, experienced flipper

If something goes wrong during the course of the project, hopefully this contingency budget will cover all or most of the problem. If little or nothing goes wrong, and everything arrives on time and without complications, and you finish the project satisfactorily, then you've got 10 percent of your budget left unspent, and that amount adds to your profit. A few flippers add in more to their contingency budget.

Potential income tax savings

Before we get too deeply into this subject regarding your planning, I must offer a word of caution. Although I'll briefly cover a few items that may result in some savings in your income taxes, these are just general subjects of discussion for you to consider. They will not apply equally to everyone, and, in some cases, they may not apply to your situation at all. They are, however, items you may wish to discuss with your accountant as you do both your tax planning and the preparation of your tax returns.

I'll deal only with potential savings here from the certain areas of soft costs and tax code provisions. Hard-cost tax savings will not be discussed, as our considerations on the subject examine your profit *after* completing the flip, when hard costs will have already been taken into account.

It is very likely that most, if not all, of your soft costs will have been accounted for in arriving at the profit figure for your project. One that may not have been included, depending on timing, is property tax. If your property tax on the flipped project is settled at close of escrow through your title company, you will likely have a net figure that, through the close of the property's sale, you will have paid, and be left with your profit.

However, if you are in a jurisdiction where taxes are settled only on a certain tax date, and that date comes after you have sold the property, you'll pay the tax. Because it's an expense related to the project, you will probably be able to deduct the property tax amount when doing your income tax returns.

There are a couple of other very specialized areas that could yield major income tax savings or deferments. They are very limited and very specific, but, if you qualify, they are definitely worth considering. Your accountant can advise you.

The first of these is the 1031 Exchange. So named because of the specific section number of the Federal Income Tax Code, the 1031 Exchange allows the taxpayer, if he or she qualifies, to defer, potentially indefinitely, all taxes on any profits in real estate. Usually used by real estate investors who are buying and holding real property for investment purposes, it is conceivably available to someone doing property flips as well.

Basically, it works as follows. The property investor—in this case, you—sells at a profit a previously purchased piece of property. Once the sale of that property is closed, the investor then has a total of 180 days to close the purchase of a replacement property that costs at least as much or more than the one just sold.

The investor must also have identified the property ultimately purchased as the replacement within the first 45 days of the 180-day period. He or she has a maximum of three choices of replacement property, one of which *must* be the ultimate purchase.

Failure to identify or close the sale within the stipulated time periods renders the exchange void for tax purposes, and the investor is liable for the tax in that tax year, just as if no

Moneysaver

Consider the 1031 Exchange to defer capital gains tax on your project's profits.

exchange had even been attempted. Due to the somewhat complicated details that can be involved in such a set of transactions, this is a procedure that you should *discuss carefully and thoroughly* with your accountant.

Another possible area of savings on your income tax is what I'll call professional qualification. If you do flipping as your main business, as opposed to something you do from time to time as what will likely be considered a form of investment by the tax authorities, you may fall under the qualification of being a professional doing flips as a business. This may allow you more benefits than merely doing it as an additional source of income or investment. Again, the details are complex, and should be very carefully and fully discussed with your accountant.

Profits: your "take-home"

At this point in your planning you've arrived at the finish. After careful thought, analysis, and planning, you've established a budget, made contacts and possibly contracted with contractors, and very likely commenced your search for the property that you'll flip. If you've come this far and are continuing into the acquisition of the subject property, you've finished up the paperwork with a profit figure at the bottom.

Pay careful attention to that budget as you progress through your project. You'll want to do so because you may, as your project develops, want or need to make some changes in the project to remedy unexpected challenges or take advantage of unexpected opportunities. When you finish the project and actually pocket your profit, you'll have a number of options as well. We'll look at these more closely in the final chapter of the book.

Just the facts

- When assembling your budget, be sure you consider all costs—hard as well as soft.
- Soft costs include pre-construction non-physical expenses for the project: legal, architectural, accounting, financing, and insurance.

- Hard costs include labor and materials expense for the project.

- Because "something" is almost always certain to happen, *always* include a contingency expense of at least 10 percent as a budget item.

- Every situation is different, so be sure to discuss potential income tax savings strategies with your accountant.

Acquiring the Property

GET THE SCOOP ON...
Assessing the condition of the property ▪ Design
and size considerations ▪ How age can affect
building codes ▪ The importance of location ▪
Project timing and market timing ▪ Work with a
Realtor or do it yourself?

PART II

Locating the Right Property

O kay, so you've gotten to the next major step in your flip—selecting the right property. If you've previously done flips, you already know what I'm about to say. If not, it's the first piece of cautionary advice I have to offer at this point in the process. There never will be the "perfect" property for your flip. This holds true no matter which of the three types of flip you plan to do. Something will always be just a bit different than what you want, or a tiny bit too small—or large—for your preferences. The neighborhood will be good, but if this house were just a few blocks farther down the street, it would be so much better.

Nevertheless, you have to start somewhere, so don't get too hung up on this fact of life. You can search for, and probably find, an excellent property to flip successfully. When you finish it, only you will ever know what you thought was "wrong" with it when you began. Assuming the item you felt was "wrong" wasn't an actual physical defect that would have to be disclosed to a buyer, no one need ever know, and you have no reason to reveal your original feelings on this item to anyone.

Condition of the property

The first issue to consider is the existing condition of the property you're planning to acquire. This can be looked at in either of two ways: Decide which type of flip you're going to do first, and then search only for properties that are conducive to that type of flip; or look at all properties, regardless of their condition, and then decide what type of flip you'll do based upon the condition of the property you finally decide to acquire. Each school of thought has its proponents and opponents.

I prefer to first decide what type of flip to attempt, and then search for the appropriate property. The reasons for this are fairly simple. It cuts down on the number of properties you'll likely have to look at before making your purchase. Reducing the number of candidate properties will also, in most cases, save you time, and, obviously, money. Finally, it allows you to get more focused on the project you intend to do and avoid distracting yourself with other options that likely won't be suitable for your project.

The only instance in which looking at fewer candidate properties can add time to the process of acquiring the right property is in situations where the market has a smaller-than-usual inventory from which to select. In these situations, you may find yourself taking longer to acquire a property, or, in some cases, re-evaluating your decision as to which type of flip you do.

For example, if you want to do a cosmetic flip, but months of looking haven't produced a suitable property for cosmetic flips, but you *have* seen a few that would do very well as intermediate

---

 Bright Idea

Keep your expectations realistic. Remember that no potential flip will ever be perfect!

Watch Out!

Regardless of what type of property you seek, the more deteriorated its condition, the more work you'll have to do and money you'll need to spend. The condition of a property will indicate to you the type of flip for which it's best suited.

flips, you may, after careful consideration, decide to do an intermediate and save the cosmetic for another project. Again, however, remember that no property will be perfect, so when you decline a particular candidate, do so on more specific bases than its perceived perfection for the project.

Remember also that right now we're talking only about locating the property. It's entirely possible, as I'll discuss in the next chapter, that the property you first select may not ultimately end up being the one you actually acquire and with which you complete the project.

Assuming you follow the same preference I have in property location—search based on a planned type of flip—condition will have a great deal to do with what you ultimately attempt to acquire. If you're planning on a cosmetic flip, you don't even want to see a property that's almost falling down, or has major roof or foundation issues, or that may be fine structurally, but obsolete as to its present use options. Conversely, if you plan to do a total gut, a house that's structurally in excellent condition with all the right number and location of rooms, including exactly the currently desired amenities, and that only needs updating of its paint and kitchen tile, is obviously not the candidate for you.

As I'll discuss later in this chapter, whether you search for a property yourself, use a Realtor, or combine the methods, you'll tailor your search accordingly.

Design and size

The next subjects to consider in your search are those of design and size. Don't bite off more than you can chew! You can always redo Buckingham Palace on your next project. There are few things worse than getting midway through your project only to find out that had you been a bit more conservative in your original choice of acquisitions, you wouldn't now be facing a large extra expense because the style is just obsolete enough, or the size of the structure is a few hundred square feet more than you'd planned on, so that even your fabulous plans are likely not going to result in the profits you expected. Again, caution when locating the property, coupled with a careful examination of all of its aspects and details, can save you a great deal of aggravation down the road.

There are also other things to be careful about. When choosing a house, be sure that it is one that fits the character of the neighborhood. For example, don't pick a huge three-story English Tudor if every other home in the area is a single-story ranch. While you're at it, keep the style of the house. Improving it is fine, but changing it from a Tudor to a Mediterranean is a waste of your time and money, and will likely either cost you most, if not all of your profit, or result in a longer time period to get it sold.

Another thing to beware of is paying for details in the existing house that you do not want in your finished product. A flipper I know, Robert, notes that if you don't plan on having a pool in your completed flip, you shouldn't buy a house that has one. This is because you'll probably pay more for the house because it has a pool, and then you have to either change your plans to accommodate it, or fill it in to get rid of it. Either way, you'll be spending money that you had budgeted elsewhere. Similar situations include stone walls surrounding the property when you want an open feel.

> 66 Make sure your finished flip isn't the most expensive house on the block. It should fit in, not outclass the neighborhood. 99
>
> —Robert, experienced flipper

The age factor

The age of the property is another important factor to consider, for a number of reasons. Obviously, design and style change over time, and what was popular in the 1950s may not be now (unless it's a unique style that has its own loyal following regardless of year; examples of this are Victorian and Eichler styles).

The older a building is, the more likely it is that a higher percentage of the building will have deteriorated to the point of needing major repair or total replacement. This means more expense for you. Obviously, if you're doing a total gut anyway, this may be less of a concern than if you're planning on updating only a kitchen and bath or doing just a cosmetic flip. However, you should always pay attention to a structure's age.

Another way that age can be a major factor in what you are able to do, and how much it may cost you, is building code changes. In California, for example, there are certain code requirements to counter or decrease possible earthquake damage that have come into code as time and experience have shown them to be necessary. These include such items as bolting the structure to the foundation to avoid a house sliding off the foundation when the ground shakes, possibly causing its total destruction. Also, modern codes often require shear walls be placed across the framing to lessen the effects of earth movement on the vertical structure of a home. If the house you're considering for your flip was built before the current codes requiring such items were in effect, you may find you have to comply with them as part of your flip—which means increased expense.

Other parts of the country have similar local construction safety items that have been written into their codes as the experience of natural disasters has led to the codes' updating. In the central part of the nation, for example, some codes have sections to try to alleviate flood damage.

Areas where temperature extremes, hot or cold, are the norm may have added special requirements on type of construction material used, or what insulation, roofing, or windows may be used in new construction, including that done in a flip.

My own house in California is a good example of how changes in codes can affect flip costs. The original house was a one-story two-bedroom house built in 1950, and added on to in the mid-1970s. We acquired it in the late 1970s and in the early 1990s, added a second story. Among the things we had to do to our new construction that the earlier portions of the home did not, and do not now have, was building shear walls on all the new framing for the upper floor and the portion of the lower story remodeled to support that second story, as well as the addition of interior sprinklers on all of the new construction. These changes added almost $20,000 to the cost. It could have been worse: Had the square footage of the addition been just a couple of hundred square feet larger, the latest codes would have required we retrofit sprinklers in all of the previously existing parts of the house.

It's all about location

You've probably heard the adage that the most important thing in real estate is "Location, location, location." Nowhere is this truer than in the selection of a property to flip. Carefully consider both the neighborhood where a candidate property is located, and the candidate property's location within the neighborhood. If the neighborhood has a poor image in the area—due to its location, the local crime rate, or some natural topographical or geographical problem, such as hills, marshland, or a river—it will still have that status no matter what kind of wonderful creation you establish on the site. While such a problem will probably enable you to buy the property at a lower cost than if it were in a better location, it will also lessen the amount you can get when you sell your finished project. There's not much you can do about that. You may find it a wise choice to just stay away from that area for now.

Speaking of location, there is another thing to keep in mind. You may have an excellent neighborhood for your flip, and a great candidate property. Yet one unalterable item can make the project location a poor one, or cost you money when you sell. That is if the location you choose is very close to a busy street, bus stop, or schoolyard. All of these are noisemakers, and, while most people recognize the need for such things, they also may not want them within earshot of their home.

On the other hand, if the only location problem is that the neighborhood is great, and has amenities and topography that everyone is seeking, but your candidate is below the neighborhood standards, it may be a prime candidate for your consideration. You may have a larger return on investment (ROI) on a property that is below the general standards of a neighborhood. This situation is what I call the "yuck factor": Your first reaction upon seeing the property may be to scream "yuck" at the top of your lungs. The paint may be peeling, or it may have a few broken windows or a totally unappealing overgrown lawn and weed-strewn garden. Like the first house I ever bought, it may have a driveway that is so broken up it looks as if a war had been fought there. However, all such factors can offer potentially a great project candidate. Very likely such a house will cost less than its neighbors on the same street, and, once completed, sell for top dollar.

Such disrepair often continues inside the house. Maybe floors need refinishing, or the bathroom tile is 50 years out of date. Perhaps the color and design of paint and wallpaper are similarly from the distant past. This can all offer a great potential project candidate.

An excellent example of this is an intermediate flip done by clients of mine. Buying a dated, unattractive property from the estate of an elderly lady, my clients mowed the lawn, totally redesigned and replanted the gardens, remodeled the kitchen and baths, added carpet, and repainted inside and out. Their profit was a bit over $43,000 in just over four months. That profit figure, by the way, is after all costs, including commissions paid to their Realtor.

> **❝** Carefully examine the neighborhood. Assuming the house is sound, the neighborhood can be a good guide as to your chances at profitability. **❞**
>
> —Christine, experienced flipper

Done properly, the property that generates "yuck" when you first see it can lead to a chorus of "wow!" when you're finished, and, most important, make you a very nice return on your investment. Also, because you picked a property that was in a good neighborhood, but only suffered due to its own condition, you benefit in your sales price when you are finished by the fact that it's a good house in a good location.

Timing is everything

Timing is another essential factor to look at when choosing a property. There are two types of timing to consider: project timing and market timing. Both are equally important.

Project timing

Project timing is the amount of time that it takes you, from the moment you acquire your property until you complete the work on it and are ready to sell, to actually finish the flip. It doesn't include the time it took you to locate, inspect, and acquire the property, and it also does not include the time it takes you and/or your Realtor to sell the property.

This is important because it's another example of the adage that "time is money." The more time that you take in working on and completing the project, the more money it's going to cost you. The more money it costs you, the less profit you may end up with.

There is a good rule of thumb to demonstrate how extra time can increase your costs and eat into your profits. When a bank forecloses on a property, one of the reasons that it tries to get that property sold to a new owner as soon as possible is because of the costs the bank incurs by owning it. It is usually assumed that every month that a foreclosing bank owns that property, it costs the bank roughly 1.5 percent of the property's value in carrying costs. These include taxes and insurance. This same 1.5 percent estimation is a pretty good rule of thumb in calculating what it costs you to own the property while you're working on the flip. Actually, it may be a bit on the low side, as you also have interest to pay while you're using your bank loan to help pay for the costs of the flip. Putting this in more specific terms, for every $100,000 of value in the property, you're bearing the cost of $1,500 every month you hold it, not including interest. You may not be actually writing a check for that amount, but when you calculate the monthly value of your insurance and real estate taxes, you'll find it comes pretty close to this figure.

Based on all of this, it logically follows that any way you can take less time to complete the project without sacrificing the quality of work or materials will be money saved. While you won't actually be using any of the project time until you have acquired the property and begun work on it, there is no time to begin planning the allocation of this time like the period leading up to the actual acquisition of the subject property.

As part of the planning process you can investigate the time involved from ordering materials until delivery to the job site, and arrange your subcontractors' times on site accordingly. There are few more frustrating things than to either have materials on the site and remaining unused while the workers who are supposed to be performing that portion of the work are not available due to a conflict in schedule that could have been forecast months earlier, or to have the labor available on site and unable to complete the task at hand because the materials needed either haven't been delivered yet, or are on back order and won't be available for several weeks.

Certain types of materials are notorious for causing such delays. Some types of granite or marble for kitchen or bath counters fall into this category, as do custom cabinets and some

Moneysaver

Coordinate materials delivery dates and contractor availability for each part of the flip. This avoids lost time and wasted expense that shows up in the form of additional interest costs incurred while you wait. It also gets you to market sooner, possibly avoiding adverse changes in market conditions.

rarer types of wood flooring. In my own home, when we redid a kitchen, the specific type of granite we wanted for our counters, after looking for two months to decide, had to be back ordered for another six weeks due to demand for that particular granite. We were able to cut this period down to four weeks by placing non-binding orders at a half-dozen different local wholesale suppliers and grabbing the first to arrive. But the point here is such issues as popularity of a particular item, or its scarcity, can raise hell with a timeline for the project, and this can sometimes be avoided by advance planning. One way to possibly cut down this type of time loss is to try and stay with stock items as much as possible. While your personal taste might dictate more exclusive material in your own personal home, it usually won't be necessary for a flip.

Market timing

Market timing is the relationship of your project to what is going on in the local real estate market. In a strong sellers' market, prices are likely to be rising rapidly, and doing a flip at this time could be very profitable for you. You'd probably be able to sell your completed flip for a higher price than you would in a buyers' market. If the market presently has a lower-than-normal inventory for your type of property, again, you have a better opportunity to make money than if the market is glutted and inventory is taking longer to sell. This is just another example of the old supply-and-demand factor at work.

Extremes of the market can be factored into your overall planning regarding both timing the initiation of your flip and, in some cases, whether to commence a new project at all.

Clearly, if the market is dead with no signs of any improvement for the next several months, or the economy is in a recession and few people are investing in new or newly redone homes, the timing of the market is probably telling you to step back and wait until things show signs of improving.

Another aspect of market timing is the time of year that you do your project. If you're buying at a time when the weather is mostly bad (depending on where you live), the issue you have to address is how soon the weather usually improves. There's nothing wrong with buying the project property during bad weather and using the rest of the rainy or snowy season to do the entitlements and final design work, leaving you to commence hard on-site work just as soon as the weather breaks. However, buying the property in late autumn when bad weather is likely to arrive very soon, causing limited, if any, work to be possible, can be very costly in terms of extra money spent on interest and other soft costs while you wait two or three months for the weather to improve.

Perhaps your market has certain times of year when properties sell faster than in other times. If you can time your project to take advantage of those times, you can save money on the carrying costs and possibly sell for a higher price, all adding up to more profits and a better return on your investment.

A good example of this is my own market in northern California. We have two good selling times of year. They consistently occur at the same time, differing from one year to the next only by the intensity of the market in terms of sellers versus buyers. The first time of year is early spring, from the start of February through mid-May. The market's intensity determines

---

 Watch Out!

In severe weather areas, a partially completed house is much more likely to suffer weather-related damage in the winter than in a warmer part of the country. This damage means one thing: more expense for you. That reduces your profit.

Bright Idea

Time your finished project to come to market during the market's usual "hot" sales periods.

how deeply into June and July this continues. The second time of year is early to mid-fall, starting around Labor Day and ending just before Thanksgiving.

Homes do sell during the winter holiday season and in July and August, but comparatively very few. At these times, most buyers are not thinking of buying houses. They're usually focused on other matters. Clearly, one would try to bring a completed flip to market in this section of the country at some time other than these periods.

Searching for properties

After completing your planning as to the size, condition, and location of the property you are going to flip, and planning both your work and market timing, it's time to go out and obtain the property. The first step is to search the market. There are two ways to do so:

- Use a Realtor.

- Do it yourself (DIY).

My preference is the former. Even if you're very experienced and an expert at searching for property, you can't possibly do as good a job in finding the appropriate property by yourself as you can working with a good Realtor. The operative words here are *working with*. The Realtor will search the market for whatever you tell him or her you're seeking, but it is imperative that you not only view any candidates that are turned up in your search, but that you also provide your agent with explicit input as to each property you are shown. It is through this give-and-take between you and your Realtor that the agent can hone in on and find the desired property for your project.

Using a Realtor

With a Realtor, you'll agree on specific parameters you seek at the start of your search. A good agent will get as specific a set of parameters as possible for your search before ever actually looking for property. The exact process will vary somewhat from agent to agent, but it will be very detailed. Before we ever take a client to look at property, we go over every conceivable detail, and even then, on the first trip to view properties, throw in one or two that are diametrically opposite to the buyer's expressed preferences. That's because on occasion a buyer will want to purchase something that's completely at odds with what the buyer told us he or she wanted. As your search continues, you may find yourself adjusting these parameters a bit, depending on market conditions or what you are learning from what you're seeing as you examine the market, but your parameters will be used by the agent to direct the search.

Using the latest technology, it is likely that the agent will combine the Multiple Listing System (MLS) with various processes such as e-mail, the Internet, and IDX. The last of these, IDX, is a software-based system in which prospective buyers can access the local MLS either directly or through their agent's Web site and view the listings just as soon as the agent is able to access them. This lessens the likelihood of a good candidate property falling through the cracks by allowing both the buyer and the Realtor to see the latest properties to come to market.

With the combination of the Web-based MLS, e-mail, new software to expose property to the market, and digital photography, using an agent who is technologically proficient can be an unmatched blessing in getting your ideal property when and where you want it. Technology goes beyond the mere e-mailing of property information. Today, using digital photography with the Web and e-mails, an agent can take "virtual tours" of any properties matching a buyer's parameters and e-mail entire video tours of the properties to the buyer for his or her consideration.

Bright Idea

The Cyberstars total only 200 agents out of 1.2 million licensed Realtors nationally, but they are as cutting edge as any group of Realtors can be in using technology to best serve their clients. A full list of these agents and their locations is available online at www.cyberstars.net.

Another benefit of using a Realtor is that once you pick a geographic area for your flip, you can similarly customize your choice of Realtor. Using one who specializes in the area you've chosen will usually produce quicker results because the agent is usually "wired" into all of the conditions of that local market and can find things for you quicker than someone who isn't as market-focused.

Once properties are located through this process, the agent can arrange access for the buyer, be it one property a day or many properties a day. Another way for the agent to get the buying flipper to as many properties as possible is to analyze the list of new-to-market properties on that week's agent "tour" and have the buyer go to the brokers' open houses on the tour, thus getting in to the properties as soon as they're available on the market.

Doing it yourself

The other option in searching the market is to do it yourself, or DIY. If this is your first foray into the market, or if you've done a little in the real property market previously but are still relatively inexperienced, I have only one word of advice for you: *don't!* There is no way you can possibly search for property as effectively as an experienced Realtor can. Even if you read the open house ads regularly, check out the fancy full-color real estate magazines, and log on to the Web numerous times daily, you cannot mount nearly as effective a search by yourself as you can working with a Realtor.

However, if you *are* experienced in the real estate market, you may be able to function very well without the services of a

Moneysaver

By using a Realtor you'll be using the time of an expert who will focus on the type of property that fits what you told the agent, while filtering out properties that don't. In other words, you'll probably save a lot of time. As the cost is the same either way—the agent's paid by the seller—why not take advantage?

Realtor. Based on your experience, you will know how to search for property, combining the availability of open houses, property ads, Web sites, and the MLS. Whereas it was just a few years ago that *only* Realtors had access to the MLS, today, virtually everyone can obtain such access. With it, if you're experienced, you can function without a Realtor. You should also be able to write your offer, negotiate any counteroffers from the seller, review disclosures, and get the purchase closed without using an agent. However, remember: All of this assumes you have experience in the process.

Just the facts

- Pick a house whose size fits the type of project and budget you're planning.
- The older a house is, the more potential issues may exist— both in its condition and as it relates to more recent code changes.
- Make sure your project design conforms to the predominating ones in the neighborhood, and avoid making your house the most expensive on the street.
- Carefully plan your project timeline to avoid costly delays.
- Plan your project to allow completion as soon as reasonably possible, and to coincide with the best selling seasons in your locale.
- When searching for a property, it's best to work with a Realtor unless you have experience in the real estate market.

GET THE SCOOP ON...
What to consider before making the offer ▪
Making a counteroffer ▪ Review of seller's disclo-
sures ▪ Physical inspections of the property ▪
Discussions about permitting issues

Chapter 7

Buying the Property

Now that you've spent time searching for the property and probably eliminated some potential sites for your project for any number of reasons, you've finally found a property that appears to suit your needs, budget, and desires. This may be the first property you've felt strongly enough about to want to make an offer on, or it may have already been preceded by one or more properties that, for one reason or another, failed to make the cut and proceed to closing.

In any event, in actually buying a property there are four main processes to go through before you become the legal owner: making the offer, due diligence, financing, and closing. I'll discuss the first two in this chapter, while financing your purchase will be covered in Chapter 8 and closing in Chapter 9.

Making the offer

When making the offer, there is more than just the price of the property to consider. While price clearly is a very important factor, it is far from the only thing to consider. Other items you will have to consider before making the offer include what contingencies, such as inspections and loan approval, you'll want to include in the offer, and how much time will elapse from acceptance of your offer by the seller to the closing of the transaction.

Pay as little as possible

When making the offer, the most obvious thing to attempt to do is to buy the property for as little as possible. Every penny you save at the start increases your profit at the end. So when you put a dollar value on the property in your offer, you must remain as faithful to your budget as possible. A number of factors come into play at this point, but, obviously, your search has very likely been directed only at properties whose listed asking price is at or very close to your budgeted target price.

If your budget dictated spending no more than $125,000, it would make no sense at all to be looking at houses priced at $225,000. You might reasonably have looked at homes priced $5,000 or $10,000 over your budget, figuring that in some cases the subject property may have been sitting unsold on the market for longer than the local average time on the market, or because a particular house may have known defects that will cost more to remedy and thus should cost less to buy. But, in the end, your actual price should stick to the amount you've budgeted to purchase the property.

Factor in estimated costs

At the same time you put your offer together, you should factor in your estimated costs, both hard and soft, in doing the makeover. (See Chapter 5 for more on what constitutes hard and soft costs.) When you were first viewing candidate houses, you should have not only viewed these candidates to see if they fit your parameters, but also been making notes as extensively as possible on the obvious changes that you'd be making to the property during the makeover, and then carefully estimated what those changes would likely cost you. Obviously, if the remodel costs you started coming up with greatly exceeded your budget, you would have moved on to another candidate property.

Soft costs were probably a little more specific going in because you likely had a quote from your architect to do the plans and blueprints, and the fees from your accountant and attorney were very likely already billed for the preliminary work they'd already completed to get you into your project.

Condition of the market

Another factor to consider in putting an actual price on your offer has nothing to do with your remodel or soft costs, and very little to do with the building's condition itself. It is a more intangible factor, but, in certain cases, every bit as important as the others I've already discussed. This is the condition of the market at the time you make the offer.

If the market is a stable one, with prices only gradually rising, a balance between buyers and sellers, and a normal inventory of properties available on the market, it is very possible to make your offer for the asking price, or, in certain cases, even a bit lower than the asking price. For instance, if the property has been on the market for more than a few weeks with no offers, you may be able to get it for less than what the seller is seeking. Similarly, if the market is heavily favoring buyers, you may be able to successfully purchase the home at a price below that being sought by the seller, unless he or she has already taken the market conditions into consideration when pricing the home.

On the other hand, in a very hot sellers' market there may be strong competition for homes of the type in which you're interested. You may find more than one other buyer competing for "your" home. A home "made to flip" in my neighborhood just went 27.4 percent over asking price and had ten offers. In cases with this potential for competition, you may find yourself faced with a difficult decision. Should you go above your planned purchase amount, and, if so, how much over? You may decide that since the market is very hot for sellers—and projections are

Watch Out!

The buyer competition from people wanting to buy property for their personal residence may cause them to be willing to pay a lot more than the asking price. Don't allow yourself to be pulled into that type of bidding war. If you win against this type of buyer, you may have just eaten up all of your planned profit.

for it to remain that way for at least as long as it takes you to complete your remodel—you can afford to go over the budgeted purchase amount by a little bit, and add it on to your projected sales price when you go to sell. If successful, doing this would maintain your profit in actual dollars.

You may also decide, after careful consideration and discussion with your Realtor, that you'll pass on this house and keep looking, or, if you do make an offer, to go no higher than a specific amount above your budgeted amount.

Contingencies

In addition to price, you must decide what contingencies you'll have in your offer and how long you want to have until you remove them. The most common contingencies to an offer made by a buyer are for due diligence and for loan approval. Due diligence includes any physical inspections of the property as well as a review of any disclosures provided by the seller about the property. I'll cover this in more detail in the next few paragraphs.

Loan approval

Loan approval is just what it says. It is the time you want to be certain that your lender who's providing the financing for your project is approving the loan necessary to buy the property. In today's market, you'll be best advised to already have a loan approved, usually subject only to the appraisal of the property you want to purchase, and the details of a preliminary title report on that property. Getting pre-approved serves two purposes. It

Bright Idea

You may beat out competing buyers in a sellers' market by being pre-approved for your financing. This takes one worry off the seller's mind if he or she chooses your offer over another that's the same or a higher amount of money.

makes it easier for you to proceed with your project, saving you a few weeks to a month, in most cases, from doing it after your offer's accepted. It also gives the seller a bit more peace of mind because the seller knows when you make the offer that, subject to the appraisal and title report, he or she has an offer from a buyer who's already been approved for the financing and that the sale shouldn't fall apart over this issue. In a buyers' market, it may even make the seller accept a slightly lower offer for the property than what he or she had been asking.

Counteroffers

At this point in the process, another thing may conceivably happen. Perhaps there are other offers besides yours. Perhaps the seller likes some aspects of your offer, but not others. The seller can in these cases reject your offer, which means that you can start looking for another property, or the seller can counter your offer.

A counteroffer means that the seller is responding to your offer by specifying what items in the offer the seller would like to change, and which are acceptable. Maybe the offered price is too low, or the seller would like to reduce the time allowed for your inspection contingency to be released from the 15 days you offered to 10, or maybe you want to close the sale in two weeks and the seller wants a month. Whatever it is, the seller will provide you a written counter to your offer that tells you what the issues with your offer are and how the seller would like them changed. You can accept the changes, counter the seller back, or reject the changes entirely and move on.

Due diligence

Counteroffers or not, assuming that at some point you have an agreed deal, you will move on to the second process in the purchase of the property: due diligence. Due diligence is made up of three areas: review of seller's disclosures, physical inspections of the property, and discussions with governmental bodies on permitting issues.

Seller's disclosures

Seller's disclosures are at a minimum a compilation of everything the seller *is aware of* that is negative about the condition of the property prior to his ownership as well as at present. Note I emphasized seller's *awareness*. If the seller's not aware of a problem, he or she isn't bound to disclose it to you.

Some lawsuits by buyers against sellers have further extended this obligation. These suits have held that an issue with the property must be disclosed to a buyer if the seller is aware of it, *or should have been aware* of it. A good example of this is toxic mold, one of the hottest issues for disclosure at the current time. If the seller of the property had an ongoing roof leak, or a major plumbing leak that lasted for a bit of time, he or she may not know if any mold actually exists behind the sheetrock or up in the attic crawl space. But, because mold is exacerbated by moisture, the seller should have assumed that it *might* exist and have it investigated to see if it had formed. The leading mold liability case in Dripping Springs, Texas, was just such a case. For the seller's non-disclosure, a court held him liable for many millions of dollars.

Usually, the seller will provide you with a list of all such items, some so obvious that you may have not only already noticed them, but even factored them into the amount of your initial offer.

Other problems may not be so obvious. Perhaps the furnace works only sporadically, a fact that you're not likely to be aware of by simple observation because it's the middle of a very hot

Watch Out!

Aside from being problems that must be dealt with that will cost money, both mold and faulty furnaces can be LETHAL. Some molds are highly toxic and faulty furnaces can emit carbon monoxide.

summer at the time you're making the offer for the property. During your inspections, you may discover this fact, but the seller already knows this—it's his property and he's suffered through the last few winters at the mercy of this recalcitrant heating system. The faulty furnace would be included on the seller's list of disclosures on the property's condition for your information.

Maybe the roof has leaked this past spring. Again, unless there are water stains on the ceiling, it's not an item you'd be likely to notice. But the seller knows about it, and must disclose it.

You'll note that at the start of this discussion I said the seller's disclosure at a minimum would include any defects known to the seller about the condition of the property. Keep in mind these two points:

1. Property defects may extend beyond the actual physical condition of the property. These can include noisy neighbors, existence of nearby railroad tracks or major roadways, proximity to schools and garbage dumps, and others too numerous to name.

2. In today's litigious society, sellers are often advised by their Realtors to disclose any information that could affect the property even if it is not physically part of the property.

A good example of this situation is found in northern California, where in recent years a fungus has appeared that, relatively quickly, kills oaks and a number of other trees. So far, little has been found to be successful in deterring this fungus. Most sellers in the area are urged by their Realtors to include in their disclosure a document informing buyers that, while the seller isn't aware of any trees on the subject property that are infected, they could be because of the spread of the fungus, and the buyer is being made aware of the potential problem.

The latter of these additional disclosure points is any item or potential item in the surrounding area that could adversely affect the property's condition or future salability. A good example of this would be a buyer moving across the country and buying a home in a nice neighborhood. What the buyer doesn't know, and the seller hasn't told him or her, is that the local municipality has just received approval from the FAA to construct a commuter jetport about a quarter of a mile away in the next several months, and the projected flight path will be right over the house. It doesn't have to be anything as dramatic as a new jetport, however. It could be something as simple as a change in the local school districts, or a new bond assessment for care of the neighborhood's trees.

You'll be provided with a sheaf of documents, many of them on detailed, easy-to-read forms, by the seller that detail all known defects and conditions that may affect the property. They may also include any past defects that have been remedied by the seller. In this case, the seller may state that the furnace malfunctioned or the roof leaked, but it was repaired, and include the name of the contractor who made the repair as well as copies of the receipts for the money spent on the remedial work.

Review these documents with care. Go over anything that seems to be an issue, and ask questions of the seller. This process serves two purposes. First, it ensures that you are as aware of any problems, actual and potential, with the property

 Bright Idea

There is a good rule of thumb for disclosure that all sellers should follow: "If you can think of a possible issue, it's best to disclose it." Once you have completed the work on your project, you're going to be the seller, and you will have to make your list of disclosures to a buyer.

as is possible. Second, it may tell you that there are enough serious issues with your flip candidate that it may be a good idea to dump this property and move on before you're stuck with the seller's problems on top of the work you'd planned to do on the property.

Physical inspections

The second part of due diligence is physical inspections of the property. At a minimum, these should include a termite or pest inspection and a contractor's inspection.

Pest inspection

As the name suggests, the pest inspection looks for evidence of active or past infestations of pests that can damage the property or be a health hazard. This inspection usually costs between $200 and $400. These pests usually include termites, rodents, and ants, but, depending on local conditions, may include other pests such as snakes or small animals. A pest inspection reveals only the *presence* of pests; it does not remedy the problem (with a few exceptions, which I'll discuss in a moment), although it may give an estimate of what it would cost to have another contractor handle the situation. This estimate will vary with the extent of the damage, but can be anywhere from a few hundred to tens of thousands of dollars. In one extreme case of mine, a foreclosed property had close to $250,000 in pest damage!

Assuming you do learn of such a problem, you have a choice—dump the property or proceed with the purchase. The latter would likely depend on how successful a buyer is at negotiating either a price reduction from the seller or an agreement that the seller will pay for the repairs. In this case, if the seller is willing to bear all or most of the cost, I recommend the buyer have the purchase price reduced and then have the repairs done with the money saved on the purchase. That way the buyer can afford the expense, and knows it was done properly.

Usually, the only actual remedial action a pest inspector will take is to treat exposed wood surfaces affected by some fungus

Watch Out!

Dry rot is a sign of moisture and can destroy wood; it may also be a sign to look for mold.

or insect pests with chemicals designed to kill the pest. In more extreme cases, they may also "tent" the house, a process in which the house is enclosed in a sealed tent or canopy and then chemically fumigated to kill all insect pest infestations. In this case the seller, his family, and pets must vacate the building for three to five days because the poisons are so strong they'd likely kill off the sellers along with the pests.

One other item of note on pest inspections is worthwhile here. Dry rot is a fungus that is created by anything but "dry" conditions. It is usually found where there has been a continuous dampness to the affected wood area that wets the wood, dries out, and then is again dampened, over and over. This moisture encourages the fungus to take root and grow, feeding itself on the wood it is slowly but steadily destroying.

Contractor's inspection

In a contractor's inspection, everything from the roof down to the foundation, inside and out, is inspected. It includes not only the physical structure of the house, but also all systems in the house, such as plumbing, electrical, and heating, and even usually involves a check on the operating condition of appliances, air conditioning, and the furnace. Not only that, but due to discoveries made during this inspection, additional inspections may be deemed advisable by other experts to determine not only what a problem may be, but what remedy is recommended and how much it will cost. A typical contractor's inspection costs between $400 and $700, although in some areas it may be a bit more or less. Also, some inspectors may charge a little more than the "normal" going rate in an area. One inspector I know of in northern California, for example, charges about $1,000 for the basic contractor's inspection.

Although it's not required, it's strongly recommended that the buyer be present during the inspections. This is because the inspector can point out to you items as they are discovered and explain to you what the importance of the issue may be, whereas in the written report, all you have is the description of the problem without any clarification that you would likely get if you were present at the inspection. Additionally, due to liability issues, an inspector will often go overboard in describing a problem in his or her report, whereas in person he or she might say it's not as serious as the report will make it appear.

Once the contractor's inspection has been completed, it may have exposed enough issues that additional inspections of a particular type are requested. For example, a leaky roof may require a roofer's inspection to bid the repair. A balky furnace may require the services of a heating contractor to inspect it and find out how severe the problem is. Swimming pools and hot tubs are usually outside the scope of a contractor's inspection and thus require their own inspection. Sometimes, slope of a lot or evidence of standing water may indicate that an inspection by a soils or

> 66 When evaluating your inspections, keep in mind what sorts of changes you planned for the house anyway. For example, if you were planning to replace all of the galvanized plumbing with new copper pipes, don't worry about the leaky pipes that the inspector found. If you were always planning to put in new appliances, don't worry about the fact that one of the burners on the stove doesn't work. The seller has no idea what you were planning, so you can always try to use these defects to negotiate a lower price. 99
>
> —Robert, experienced flipper

drainage engineer is in order. A bulging retaining wall is usually an indication that an engineer should look at it. The list of possible specific inspections goes on and on, but these few examples should explain the point.

Each of these inspections is outside the cost of your basic contractor's inspection. Depending on the nature of the extra inspection, there may be a charge made by that inspector, or there may not be. Usually, an engineer coming out to not only inspect but also write a report citing the problem and its recommended remedy charges a fee for his or her work. Some contractors doing specific types of inspections—electrical, plumbing, or heating—may also charge for their time. However, some of these types, as well as those such as roofers and pavers, may not charge for their inspection and instead bid for the work, on the understanding that they will do the work recommended for the price quoted in their bids. A few of these will charge for the inspection, but deduct that amount from the cost to do the work if you use that contractor for the job.

Discussions with permitting authorities

The third type of due diligence is discussing your plans as they relate to the specific property with the local permitting authorities. This is vital because no matter how fabulous your plans are and no matter how well they fit the property you're acquiring, they're meaningless if you can't get permits to do the work. Remember, the longer these permit applications and processes take, the more it's costing you, in interest charges if nothing else. So it's very important to try to assess your ability to get the necessary permits before you go forward to closing your acquisition. While it is highly unlikely that you'll actually receive permits before you own the property and have finished plans to submit to the authorities, permitting authorities can at least give you some idea of your likelihood of success in this area through detailed conversations of what property you have in mind and what you'd like to be able to do on it. For example, they can tell you the limits on size of living area or the setbacks required on a particular piece of property. They can advise what, if any, restrictions exist on hill cuts that you may envision for terracing the lot.

You may find out that for a particular size project, you must have a certain number of off-street parking spaces. If the number is three and you only have room for one, you clearly have a choice—change your project, move on, or go forward with the knowledge that you'll likely have to fight an appeal of the planner's denial through a higher governing authority, in the latter case spending more money in the process.

For example, where I live, about 15 years ago the local planning and building departments in most of the towns, nearly simultaneously, created a new hurdle for builders. In response to concerns of people buying older homes, tearing them down, and then replacing them with new homes so much larger that they were totally out of context with the surrounding neighborhood, the authorities established "Floor Area Ratio" allowances, which limit the living area size to a specific percentage of the area of the lot. One square foot over and you are denied your permit.

New rules such as this, as well as long-standing ones, are the reason to have friendly discussions with your local planning or building authorities. It just may save you a lot of time and aggravation in the end. Clearly, the rules that affect your planned project will differ somewhat according to which type of flip you plan to do. If it's a cosmetic flip, you'll likely have the fewest permit issues with which to be concerned. On the other hand, if a total gut is what you've got in mind, you'll have the largest number of code and permitting issues to confront. You'll possibly even be faced by limitations created by "grandfathering" and the results of giving up grandfathered exceptions. That's a topic I'll discuss in greater detail in Chapter 12.

There is another factor that permitting sometimes confronts. That is the NIMBY ("not in my back yard!") neighbor. One or two neighbors can cause enough discord with the permitting authorities that your permits can be delayed for months and force expensive changes to your plans. Such opposition is difficult to predict at best. However, your conversation with the permitting authorities may result in your becoming aware of any "difficult" neighbors in the immediate area who have obstructed prior projects.

Just the facts

- Make your offer based on your careful physical assessment of the property and how well it matches your planned project.

- Carefully review the seller's disclosures for any potentially costly defects that could derail your flip.

- Attend all your inspections. You may learn more than you would by just reading the reports.

- If major damage is discovered in the inspections, consider negotiating the estimated costs of repair off of the purchase price.

- Discussion with permitting authorities can indicate well in advance whether or not your planned project will have difficulty getting approved.

GET THE SCOOP ON...
Financing through an institutional lender ▪
Using a mortgage broker ▪ Seller carry-back ▪
Self-financing options ▪ The advantages of
financing in advance

Financing Your Purchase

Chapter 8

There are three possible methods to finance the acquisition of your project property: using an institutional lender, working with a mortgage broker, and having the seller carry all or a portion of the financing debt. The first of these options further divides into two possibilities, although in the end you still have a loan from an institutional lender—a bank, savings and loan (S&L), or credit union.

A fourth alternative also exists, although it isn't "financing" in the classic sense of the word. This is using your own assets exclusively to finance the purchase.

Institutional lenders

There are two ways to go about seeking financing from this type of lender. You can apply individually to a particular bank, savings and loan, or credit union. With this method, you submit an application to each and every lender you think you may wish to do business with, although usually one at a time. The

Moneysaver

In some cases, you may get a break on the interest rate or loan fees if you already have a relationship with a particular institution.

way you choose which of the thousands of potential lenders in this class to deal with can be as varied as the number of institutions that exist. Perhaps you have your savings or checking account with a particular bank or S&L. It makes sense to you, then, to apply there for your financing.

On the other hand, your choice of lender may be based on a particular special deal the lender is offering to attract new borrowing customers. Maybe it's a special rate for new loans, or reduced fees for a certain type of loan program. In any event, if it sounds attractive, you may apply at that institution for your financing.

Another way you may choose a particular lender is through a referral by someone you know and trust—perhaps a family member or colleague who's had a long and satisfactory experience with that particular lender. Obviously, if you or someone you know has done well at a particular source of funding, it would raise your level of comfort in seeking financing for your project.

Financing terms

This brings us to the terms of the financing. Three things need to be considered at this juncture:

- The amount of the loan

- The costs of the loan

- The loan terms (interest rate, fees/points)

The first, loan amount, can be handled in either of two ways: strictly enough to complete the purchase with a separate loan to finance the remodeling expense, or one loan that encompasses both parts of the project. The latter is often the more

Watch Out!

Find out if any prepayment penalty is required as part of the note. There's nothing worse than finishing your project ahead of schedule—and it does happen on occasion—only to find that when you pay off the loan, the lender hits you with a penalty of as much as six months' interest for paying it off early.

convenient, with a specific amount of the overall financing specifically detailed to buy the building, and that amount of debt then being rolled over and added to the financing required for the flipping construction.

Regarding loan costs, the interest rate will be whatever the interest market is offering at the time, but even there you have options. Will you do an amortizing loan, paying both principal and interest on some specific detailed schedule, or can you obtain a loan that requires only interest until you complete and sell the project? Obviously, the latter is more in your favor as far as short-term cash flow is concerned, because it means you'll have to lay out less cash to the lender during the time you're working on the project than you would if the loan were even partially amortized.

As far as the tenor of the note is concerned, remember when you're negotiating the terms—you're not planning to keep the property as your residence. You don't need a traditional long-term mortgage. Obtaining financing that allows you time to do the work and complete the project, as well as a reasonable time thereafter to market the finished property, should be a more proper term for the loan.

Cross-collaterization

Some lenders, particularly in the case of relatively inexperienced flip borrowers, will try to cross-collateralize their loans. This means that they'll not only take a mortgage on the property in your project, but also one on other real property you may already own. This provides additional security in case everything

Watch Out!

Avoid cross-collateralized loans!

goes south; they foreclose and still find themselves short on the repayment of the loan. They would then foreclose on the other properties. If this subject comes up, resist as strongly as you can, and if the lender insists, find another lender. Usually a mortgage broker will avoid such terms as part of his or her service to you, but if you're doing your own application, the issue may arise. The situation doesn't always present itself, and, in fact, is outlawed in some states.

Cross-collateralization does not refer to personal guarantees. It is common practice for lenders to require a personal guarantee from the borrower on the loan, in addition to a mortgage on the property being acquired. This is merely a legal way to require the borrower to cover any shortfall in the repayment that foreclosure might fail to do. It is, in most cases, perfectly legal, although some states do limit its application when a mortgage also exists on the property.

California, for example is referred to as a "one action" state. This means that in California, a lender has a choice to make in the case of a default on a loan on real estate. The lender can either seize the property through foreclosure, or ignore that route and go after the borrower under his or her personal guarantee. The lender cannot do both, hence the term "one action." In such cases, lenders must carefully analyze their options and decide which method of collection best benefits their interests.

Mortgage brokers

A second way of getting a particular lending institution to finance your project is to have someone else make the approach in your behalf. A mortgage broker does just that. You sit down with the mortgage broker to discuss your financial situation and your project, and he or she submits the application to one or more lending institutions that the mortgage broker feels from experience will likely not only provide you with a loan, but be the best overall fit for you and your flip.

The best part of going the mortgage broker route is that you fill out your information once and the broker arranges to get it to as many different institutions as necessary, saving you time and aggravation. Another benefit is that, unlike a bank where you are just one in a long queue of would-be borrowers, each trying to get the bank's attention long enough to make a decision, with a mortgage broker, you have a lending professional representing your interests with the bank. Assuming the broker is one who places a regular stream of loans into the bank's portfolio, the bank is likely to respond more quickly and perhaps more favorably based on their ongoing relationship.

Which method is better?

There is no definite answer to that question. Whether you choose to work with an institutional lender or a mortgage broker depends on your particular situation. If you have a good relationship with the bank down the street, it may be the way to go. If, on the other hand, you want to broaden your exposure to the financing market, you may find it easier to go through a mortgage broker.

In terms of the information you provide, as well as the various forms you'll complete, there's not much difference between the two. This is because the basic applications that the brokers use are usually generic forms of those that each institutional lender requires, without the specific bank or S&L's name and logo on them. The reason is simple: The mortgage broker will be presenting your application to several banks and S&Ls, and must use whatever format those institutions require.

To find a mortgage broker, you can ask for references, look in the Yellow Pages, or ask your Realtor, if you're working with one. My advice is to try the last method. Usually, your Realtor

> 66 Because of our relation-
> ship with a buyer's
> Realtor, we strive to
> always provide the
> fastest and best service
> possible. 99
>
> —Alan, mortgage broker

will know one or more good, reliable mortgage brokers as a result of his or her experience in helping clients obtain property financing that best suits their needs. I have one individual who I recommend no matter what the case. I tell my clients, "If Alan can't get you a loan, then no one can." He always does, and the buyers are always happy with the results. Your Realtor can likely do the same for you.

Seller carry-back

A third method of financing the purchase is to have the seller carry all or a portion of the financing debt. There are many reasons for this option. The buyer may have a credit problem that either prevents or limits the amount of financing he or she can obtain from an institutional lender. Or perhaps the seller offers more favorable financing terms than the banks in the area. There are also other possibilities.

In some cases, the seller not only wants to make a profit on the property he or she is selling, but would like to obtain an additional source of income from the transaction. By offering to carry a note on the property, the seller receives additional income in the form of the interest you'll be paying to him or her. Additionally, depending on the timing involved, the seller may be able to spread this income out over more than one particular tax year, allowing him or her to keep more of it after taxes. The seller also has the security of recording a mortgage to secure his or her interest in the property should you fail to pay off the note. Just as a bank or S&L would, the seller could then foreclose.

When seller financing is involved, it is a separate negotiation from the purchase contract, although the latter may depend on the former being satisfactorily negotiated. Usually the offer to

Bright Idea

If you use seller financing, make sure the financing agreement is reviewed by your attorney.

buy the property will state that financing is to be handled by the seller. The offer will either spell out the exact terms of the financing, or it will say something to the effect that financing is to be provided by the seller on mutually agreeable terms.

In the first case, the terms will be agreed upon as part of the purchase negotiations, and, assuming an agreement to sell the property is successfully achieved, be settled at that point. In the second case, you'll have an agreement to buy the property, but, due to the terms in that contract, if you and the seller fail to agree on financing terms, your deal to buy the property will likely fall apart. Working out the seller financing terms as part of the purchase agreement is far simpler, and involves less indecision as to whether or not an agreed deal is actually going to proceed.

In either situation, a promissory note is signed by the buyer, spelling out the amount of the financing, interest rate, and payments, as well as the tenor, or length of time, of the note. A mortgage is also usually completed and recorded, securing the seller's interest in the property under the financing.

Assuming it is properly completed and recorded, this seller-financed note and mortgage are just as legally binding on the parties as similar documents done under terms of bank financing would be. If you recall in Chapter 5, as part of soft expenses, I discussed your team, and mentioned an attorney. For anyone using seller financing as part of his or her purchase, this would be another place where an attorney would be involved by reviewing and possibly assisting in the drafting of the relevant documents.

Self-financing

With self-financing, you finance the purchase using your own assets. There are many ways to do this. The simplest is to take your own funds from whatever source you have. You can also use family funds, or utilize other bank sources such as equity lines of credit on real property you already own. In any of these forms of self-financing, there is a cost to you that you should weigh against the costs of borrowing the funds for the transaction.

If you're utilizing your own savings, calculate the amount of interest you'll lose by not having that money any longer. If you borrow the funds from friends or family members, or from a pre-existing equity line of credit, calculate the interest costs to you for this source of funding. In any of these situations, you can then compare the interest costs against the costs of a loan specifically for the project's acquisition. Whatever the actual dollar savings involved, those experienced in flipping property, as well as those investing in real estate, almost *always* advise against self-financing as opposed to lender financing. This is because they feel that by using a source of funds other than their own, it keeps their money available for other needs that may arise, and also allows them to be free to take advantage of other opportunities that may present themselves, opportunities that might otherwise be foreclosed to them if they'd used their own resources for a project. As I said in Chapter 1, rule number one is to use someone else's money whenever possible!

Plan financing in advance

In arranging the financing for the project, you should, insofar as possible, have the funding arranged and approved well in advance of making the purchase offer. The only obvious exception to this is in cases where you plan to make seller financing a part of the offer. Even there it is advisable to have a loan approved in advance in case you try to buy a property with seller financing and the seller is not having any part of your idea. If the seller turns you down, you're forced to move on and seek another property or come up with a loan from other sources to buy the property.

There are a couple of reasons why it's a good idea to get the financing arranged in advance. First, it's one less item to worry about once you've found the property you want to flip. With the loan already approved, you can turn your attention to other matters relating to the project and this property while you wait to close on the purchase. Second, in a sellers' market, it will make the seller more willing to consider your offer ahead of competing similar offers because the seller knows that financing is one thing he or she won't have to worry about sabotaging the sale of his property.

Usually, when a loan is approved before the specific property is located, it is approved as to the credit of the borrower, with such items as appraisal and title listed as the only contingencies to be satisfied for the lender at a later date before close of the purchase. These items are standard and will not take an inordinate amount of time to complete once the sale is pending. It usually takes no more than two or three weeks to complete an appraisal and receive a preliminary title report on the subject property. Once all of this is done, you are ready to close and take title to the property.

Just the facts

- A mortgage broker can make the process of financing easier due to his or her multiple contacts with institutional lenders.

- Protect yourself—avoid cross-collateralized loans as much as possible.

- Unless your credit is poor, avoid self-financing; it's always better to use someone else's money.

- The cheapest way to finance is usually interest-only loans for the planned duration of the project.

- Seller financing is an option that can save money over rates and fees charged by institutional lenders.

GET THE SCOOP ON...
Taking title on the property ▪ Title insurance ▪
Hazard and liability insurance ▪ Additional closing documents ▪ Other issues at closing

Paperwork and Closing

O nce your offer to acquire the property has been accepted, you enter a new phase of the process: completing the purchase by closing it. This is the time when any of your inspections that I discussed in Chapter 7 are done and when your financing is completed. Even in cases where you've secured financing well in advance of making your offer to buy the property, approval is usually conditional on such items as the property being appraised to ensure its value and having a preliminary title report to ensure that your seller has legal authority to sell it and has no hidden liens or judgments on the property that would adversely affect the title he would pass to you in the sale.

All of this occurs during the closing period. The length of this period is something that you and the seller agree on in your contract to purchase the property. The contract specifies the amount of time covered from the date you and the seller agree on terms of your purchase until you are to take title and become the owner of the property. This period also includes the contract-specified time limits for your inspections and loan approvals, as well as appraisal deadlines and your signoff on any seller disclosures, mandatory or otherwise.

Taking title

One of the most important things you will need to take care of during the closing period is how you intend to take title to the property. Legal title can be held in a number of ways, depending on your intent and needs. The simplest form is for you to take title in your own name. In this case, you are the titleholder—period.

This and all other forms of legal title are irrespective of the fact that a lender may have a mortgage on the property due to your financing of its acquisition. The existence of a mortgage does not make the bank a holder of ownership in the property. Rather, your ownership is subject to the lien that the lender places against the property as a form of security for the loan.

There are other ways of taking title, and they all depend on your desires and the status of who, in a legal sense, is going to own the property:

- Are you the sole owner?
- Are you working in partnership with one or more people?
- Is your personal or family trust going to own the property?
- Do you do flips as a regular business with a name for the entity that is the business and owns the property?

In each of these cases, a different method exists to take and hold legal title. This is an area in which your attorney, your Realtor, and your CPA can provide assistance.

Each form of title has its own unique characteristics and limits. Among the forms of title that can be used are:

- **Sole Owner:** You alone own the property.
- **Partnership:** You own the property in partnership with others.
- **Joint Tenancy:** More than one individual owns equal shares of the whole property.

- **Tenants in Common:** More than one individual each owns specific portions of the property.

- **Corporation:** A business or cooperation is set up as the legal owner of the property.

There are other possibilities, mostly variations on these, but these are the most common.

Keep in mind that if you do intend to finance the property with an institutional loan, the lender may want to lend to you as an individual. In many instances, lenders will not lend to a trust, partnership, corporation, or other entities. It depends on who the lender is and your relationship with that lender. The lender may require the purchase to go through in the name of the individual, and the individual may then record a grant deed changing the way title is held after the escrow closes. In the event the lender will allow the escrow to be closed in the name of the entity, the lender and the title company will require the supporting documentation from that entity.

Many people who make flipping a regular business establish a separate corporation or partnership for each project. In such cases, you should work closely with legal counsel to ensure that you have properly taken into account every requirement to establish and use such an entity in your state. Whatever form you choose, it is most likely that it will be the same legal entity that is doing the flip.

Once you have decided how you intend to hold title to the property, everything that follows as far as documentation and paperwork will reflect that choice. Title insurance will be issued in the name of the same legal entity. The deed you'll receive at closing will show that same legal entity as owner, and all documents will most likely either reflect this choice, or refer to it, possibly in an addendum to the specific document.

Title insurance

Title insurance is insurance for you that the legal title you hold to the property is valid and—with a few specific possible exceptions

Moneysaver

Instead of a full title insurance policy, ask your title insurance company to provide a binder for title insurance.

that I'll discuss in a moment—unencumbered. The insurance is issued by the title company on the property you are purchasing once the title company has completed an extensive search of all the public records that may pertain to the property. The records show the history of the chain of title, transfer by transfer from the first time it was transferred from one owner to another, and that the transfer was formally recorded in public records.

When you do purchase a property that you intend to sell within two years, you should purchase a binder from the title company. This is the title company's commitment to reinsure the property within two years. It's 110 percent of the base title rate, up front. When the property is sold within that time period, you will receive a credit from the title company for a portion of that title insurance previously paid. The sale escrow will have to be handled by the same title company that handled the purchase in order to honor the binder.

In some cases, these records extend far back into history. For example, in the original 13 American colonies, as well as in former Spanish colonies, some pieces of land date their titular history to original assignments from the English Crown or land grants from the King of Spain. In Louisiana, these title chains may extend to the days of Napoleon Bonaparte in the early nineteenth century.

Legal form of holding title

The most obvious item recorded in relation to the title of any property is the transfer of title from one owner to another, be it by sale, gift, inheritance, or legal settlement. However, there are other items that may well be recorded that also affect the title of a property. The first of these is a change in the legal form of holding title.

As I've already noted, there are many ways in which title can be held. Sometimes a title holder may wish to change the method in which title is held on a particular property because of a change in the owner's personal situation. Perhaps, for example, a single man owns a property and later marries. Though not legally required to do so, he wants his wife to have equal title to the property, so he has the title changed to include her as its legal owner, possibly as a joint tenant. Or perhaps, as part of a divorce settlement, a property that had been held jointly will now be owned solely by one of the spouses.

Sometimes, as a way to limit tax liability or to protect a future estate, the owners of real property will change title to be held by a trust of which the owners are the trustees. Developers and flippers often choose to own a particular property in the name of a partnership or limited liability corporation (LLC) established solely for that property for the life of their ownership of it. This form of ownership is not necessarily permanent. Changes are common even during one individual's period of ownership.

Cloud on the title

Other items can be recorded that affect a title. These are frequently referred to as a *cloud* on the title, the word "cloud" being used here in a definitely negative sense. While having a cloud on a title won't automatically preclude a sale from going forward, it will almost always prevent a title company from issuing a title

---

 Bright Idea

The benefit of having title insurance—and no bank will lend on property that can't get it—is that if a claim against your title arises and a court decides in favor of that claimant, the title insurance will pay off the claim so that you don't have to. As with fire or hazard insurance, it's one less thing you have to worry about.

insurance policy. That is because the company doesn't want to insure the validity of a title only to have someone else put forward a valid claim that he or she, instead, has a claim to the title of the same property. The title insurance company would then have to pay that claimant a hefty sum to settle the claim. This process is referred to "quieting the title."

The most common of these clouds to title are:

- Liens
- *Lis pendens*
- Notices of default

A lien can be placed on a property for any number of reasons, some of them a bit less onerous than others. The most common is when you get a mortgage to buy a property or take out an equity line on the property. The lender usually places a lien on the property as the legally recorded method of ensuring that you'll repay the debt.

However, other types of liens can be placed on a property. Used for reasons not as pleasant as the mortgage loan, these include:

- Tax liens, where the taxing authority liens your property for nonpayment of your taxes
- Judgment liens, where you have lost a lawsuit and the winner in the suit has placed a lien against the property as a way of forcing you to pay the judgment or have your property sold to help satisfy that judgment
- Mechanics' liens, which are a way for someone who has performed work on the property and not been paid to force you to pay for that work

Other types of clouds that may be recorded are also not terribly pleasant. These are the notice of default, which a lender formally records when it begins the foreclosure process on the property; and a *lis pendens,* which is the recording of a notice of legal action against you and the property.

When any of these items are found to exist on a title, the title insurance company will not issue title insurance on the property. Obviously, in the case of a mortgage lien, it is expected that that particular lien will be removed by payment of the mortgage in question at or before close of the sale, and the lien removed. However, in the other cases, it may not be so easy to remove the clouds to the title and you may want to forego the purchase of the property.

Easements

As I mentioned a few pages ago, there are other items that a title search will disclose and not insure your title against. These are not necessarily detrimental to your interests. Rather, they are issues affecting some part of title to the property. The most common of these is the easement. An easement is a form of title insofar as it conveys certain specified rights to its owner or recipient on the property that it affects. The most typical of these are utility or right-of-way easements. These basically give the owner of the easement access to the property in a specifically designated location or path over it for specific reasons. The utility easement may be for the electric company or gas company to periodically check and maintain their wires or pipes that cross the property. A right-of-way easement allows the holder of the easement right of way across the property, usually along a specifically designated route or pathway.

Because easements are granted in perpetuity, a title insurance company is not going to insure your title without taking notice of the easement and the rights it bestows on the easement holder. When the title company searches the property, the search is based upon public record. If there are questions regarding the actual property lines, easements, and so forth, the buyer may choose to have a survey done because the title insurance will not cover any disputes with regard to these issues.

Hazard and liability insurance

Another type of insurance that you will want to have on the property you plan to flip is a standard policy covering fire, storms, personal liability, and normal hazard damage. This insurance will cover you against any possible loss under the policy for all the usual hazards you might encounter on the property while you own it.

Depending on the type of flip you intend to do, you may want to discuss the necessary types of coverage with your insurance broker. He or she may be able, for example, to reduce your costs if you're doing a total gut by structuring the policy not to include fire coverage during the period when you're leveling the existing house and preparing to build the new one. Additionally, if you are in an area that is subject to natural hazards such as earthquake or flooding, you very well might want to carry the appropriate insurance for those dangers on the property.

Just as with title insurance, any institutional lender will likely require that you have coverage for these types of hazards while you own the property. From the lender's point of view, it's additional comfort that their security for the loan they made you will be repaid, and the property won't be at risk from destruction or lawsuit.

Because the property is likely to be vacant, you may find obtaining insurance more difficult than normal. However, to satisfy the lender, you'll likely have to have it. Check with your insurance broker. It may be that you have to obtain insurance at

 Watch Out!

Earthquakes, landslides, and flood damage are not covered by a normal home-owner's insurance policy. If your property is in an area where these types of natural disasters are likely to occur, consider purchasing extra insurance against these disasters. In the case of flood insurance, you may be required to carry it if you live in a federally designated flood plain.

a slightly higher than normal premium. Personal liability coverage may possibly be attachable to your own household policy.

Other closing documents

So far we've accounted for most of the documentation that will pass through the escrow before you can take title to the property: the purchase contract, title insurance, and hazard and liability insurance. A few others are also important and will be present.

Most important of these are the documents relating to your financing to acquire the property. These will usually include copies of the loan application you completed previously, a promissory note, and the mortgage document that, when recorded, effectively places a lien on the property to protect the lender. Along with these financing documents, there will very likely be a Truth in Lending statement setting out the details of the interest and fees on your loan. Also, there will be a deed to officially transfer title from the seller to you. A copy of the preliminary title report detailing any exceptions or liens on the property will be there, on which you will sign off.

Depending on the timing of the closing and local taxing dates, there may be documents relating to paying of real property tax on the property through the close date. There will also be documents for the federal government, and state, if the particular state you're in has income tax, to cover your tax information for the appropriate taxing authorities. These will be more important when you ultimately sell the property because then the issue of taxable profit on your project comes to the fore.

Most likely, you will be asked to provide some valid form of identification to the escrow officer even if he or she knows you.

 Bright Idea

Be sure to bring along some form of picture identification so that any certification or notarization that may be necessary can be handled without inconvenience or delay.

This will be notarized, verifying that your identification document has been seen by the title officer at the closing.

Other closing issues

A few other items of note on closing should be mentioned here.
These are more of an advisory thing, and likely, your Realtor will
cover them with you. One will be to make sure that the total
amount of funds you're using for the down payment has been
in escrow at least a few days before the scheduled closing date.
This will be to ensure that nothing gets held up by a lost or mis-
directed bank wire transferring such funds.

Another item to cover is the actual close date. I bring this up
because if you are using a loan as part of your purchase costs,
you would be advised against closing on the property on a
Monday, or, in the case of a long holiday weekend, on the first
day of the subsequent week. This is because the lender will fund
the loan prior to the weekend to ensure that funds are in escrow
to close on time. That's good. The only problem for you as a
buyer is that the bank is charging interest on those loan funds
from the moment it funds the loan, and you do not have the
title to the property until the following week. Thus, you are paying interest on the funds over the weekend without owning the
property. A close later in the week, from Tuesday to Friday,
avoids this.

If you are selling an investment property in the state of
California, you may be subject to a 3⅓ percent tax based upon
the sales price (not the proceeds). In the event the seller is a
non-resident foreign person, the IRS requires 10 percent of the
sales price to be paid to the IRS at the time escrow closes.

 Moneysaver

Pay less interest-—NEVER close the purchase on the first day of the week!

Just the facts

- You can take title in a number of ways—sole owner, partnership, joint tenants, tenants in common, trust—pick the one that's best for you.

- Title insurance protects your legal title from unexpected claims against it.

- If the property is in a special type of hazard zone—where earthquakes or floods are common, for example—get special hazard insurance; regular insurance won't cover you.

- Be aware of easements across the property—they are in perpetuity and are usually not covered by title insurance.

Planning the Flip

GET THE SCOOP ON...
What you need to know about permits before
getting started ▪ Where to find materials ▪ Paint
and wallpaper options ▪ Sprucing up cabinets ▪
Boosting the look with new appliances ▪ Natural
and electric lighting ▪ Using tile and stone ▪ The
importance of curb appeal

PART III

Cosmetic Flips

Chapter 10

Well, now that you own it, it's time to start creating your profit. As I've mentioned, the cosmetic flip is the easiest, quickest, and least costly type of flip you can undertake. In this chapter, I'll discuss the items most likely to be addressed in creating your flip.

For the most part, you'll find yourself focusing on surface items of décor and design. These are things like wallpaper, paint, counter tile, and plantings. Remember, you are *not* doing any major demolition or reconstruction in a cosmetic flip. You are, instead, taking a house that is solid structurally and has a good floor plan and making it look better by prettying up the surface. It's exactly like a woman putting on makeup. That is why it's called *cosmetic*.

A few words about permits

Before I discuss the details of what you must be concerned with in completing your cosmetic flip, I want to briefly mention one subject that affects *all* types of flips: permits. Chapter 12 deals with permits in much greater detail because there is so much more permitting done in relation to a total gut than in any of the other types of flips. However, each locale or jurisdiction has its own rules regarding permits and when you must apply for one. So, before you begin work on your property, talk to your local building or planning department and find out what permits, if any, you will need for your project. Then get them and, once they're in hand, proceed to do your project. It is likely that for a typical cosmetic flip you will need few, if any, permits. But ask the question, so that midway through your work—or worse, when it's completed and on the market—you are not suddenly confronted with the issue of no permits when they were required, and, as a result, facing a large penalty fee that must be paid to the local authority—or worse, in extreme cases, an order to rip out all of your new work.

Finding materials

Unless you decide to be really exotic in terms of materials for a particular reason, most of the materials in this chapter are easily accessible in almost every town and city in the country. They're as easy to obtain as going down to your neighborhood hardware, paint, or building supply store.

If there's one near you, you can also get virtually everything you'll need for a cosmetic flip at either Sears or a large home improvement store such as Home Depot. In fact, in the latter case, as you'll see in intermediate and total gut flips (discussed in Chapters 11 and 12, respectively), due to the totality of assistance in materials and advice from these stores, some projects are referred to as "Home Depot jobs."

Paint and paper

Probably the toughest part of limiting yourself to new paint and wallpaper is deciding on just the right color combination and wallpaper design. With the colors and patterns currently on the market, you have a broad choice. You can be as plain vanilla as you choose or as unique as you dare. Just remember—you are not doing this to live in the house yourself. Rather, you are

Watch Out!

Don't create a "one-of-a-kind" house. Avoid extremes of color or design. Although a unique house may truly be beautiful, you'll have a much more difficult time selling it because it will appeal to a much smaller group of potential buyers.

redoing the house to appeal to as broad a range of people, given the size and layout of the property, as possible.

Choose your colors and patterns to take advantage of some of the home's attributes. If there is already a lot of light in the house, you probably have more options for using color than if the home is a bit darker inside. Rooms that are dark need some lightening that only white or very light colors can provide. In these rooms, leave bright colors to individual accent points such as those mentioned in the next paragraphs. The best advice is to start with neutral colors and paper and then go from there. Generally avoid using anything garish or exotic, except where there is a particular area of the home that might need something a bit more interesting to enhance the feature.

Neutral, however, does not have to mean that everything must be some shade of white or beige. Using light colors can brighten up a room or an area where totally neutral would leave it looking washed out. A good example of this would be in a room with lots of windows and/or a large skylight. An alternative to this is to stick with neutral colors and accent them with color on the crown or baseboard moldings, as well as the window trim.

Another way to appeal to a wider group of potential buyers and still have some bold color is to paint one wall in a large room or open area in a bright color, and then leave the rest in neutrals. Similar things can be done with wallpaper. There are many trim papers that are applied along the tops of walls and have decorative color or design motifs to contrast with the more basic color of the rest of the wall. In the latter case, there are

Bright Idea

For the same reasons that you try to be more neutral in color selection, stay away from bold geometric designs or patterns in the wallpaper. The less design-specific you are, the broader buyer base you can potentially appeal to.

even activity- or person-specific wallpaper trim strips on the market. For example, for a children's room, trim depicting cartoon characters or children's games could be applied, while a man's den might have trim portraying outdoor scenes such as fishing or boating.

You'll also want to consider what room a particular paint is being used for. If you're in a kitchen or bath, for example, you would be wise to use something that has an easier to clean surface than basic flat wall paint. A good semi-gloss will take care of this. The trim should also be semi-gloss.

One item in wallpaper that is seeing a comeback today after being out of favor for about 20 years is grass cloth paper. There are many varieties of this type of wallpaper and, as with real grass, they also cover a broad spectrum of color and texture. As the name suggests, the wallpaper is covered with pieces of real grass or other natural material. In fact, in spite of the name, there are even a number of "grass cloth" papers that are surfaced in what amount to tiny twigs or bits of tree bark.

> **❝**Use a single shade of off-white paint throughout the house and then jazz it up when you go to sell by incorporating colorful furniture and accessories into the décor. You'll save by not having to have multiple colors mixed for you.**❞**
>
> —Robert, experienced flipper

Using this type of paper selectively can not only help in maintaining a good color scheme for the project, but also add character and detail to the house. As with paint, this can be used either for an entire room or just an accent by only covering one wall to either blend or contrast with the paint on the other walls.

If you choose paper, be aware that it is more labor intensive than paint. So, if you really are on a bare-bones budget, you may find it wiser to go strictly with paint.

Cabinet refacing

Another bit of cosmetic work involves refacing kitchen and bath cabinets. When you acquire the property, you may find you have good serviceable cabinets in the house's kitchen and baths, but think they would look much better if the style and/or visible condition of the cabinets were more appealing. Since you're only doing a cosmetic flip, replacement of the cabinets is out of the question due to time and expense. However, there is a way to make it *appear* that you have replaced the original cabinets with new ones. That is to reface them.

Refacing involves replacing or resurfacing only the doors of the cabinets. There are sources of new cabinet doors for just this purpose, and the resulting look is brand new, while the cost is, relatively speaking, dirt cheap. Using this method, you can completely change the style of cabinets, as well as their color and/or wood grain. In a few cases, you can even increase the utility of cabinets by refacing with fronts that slide up into the frames rather than opening outward.

Another way to give the effect of new cabinetry is to just refinish them with new paint or stain and then merely change the hardware. For example, you can replace boring round wooden knobs with more modern and interesting metal fixtures of Florentine brass, brushed pewter, or wrought iron, in designs of virtually any style and shape. In addition to metal, many of today's cabinet fixtures are available in such diverse materials as glass, plastic, wood, and stone. Costs of these items are nearly as varied as the choices in the items themselves. You can spend as little as a dollar or two for each fixture, or go to the other extreme and spend as much as thirty or forty dollars for a single cabinet handle

Watch Out!

When you change the handles on a cabinet, make certain that the hinges for the cabinet door match the style of your new handle. Few things look worse in the redone kitchen or bath—or more negatively impact the selling price—than something such as Florentine brass finished handles and black wrought-iron hinges.

or drawer pull. Obviously, if you're trying to save money, you would be more likely to keep things at the lower end of the range.

Appliances

You can get a good boost in your finished selling price for relatively little expenditure by installing one or two new appliances. You can get lower-end stoves, refrigerators, dishwashers, and washers/dryers from Sears or home improvement stores such as Home Depot that will complete the "brand new" and wonderful appearance you're trying to achieve. For more on this subject, see Chapter 11.

Light and bright

Another area where you can maximize your return is by ensuring that the finished house is as light and bright inside as possible. This is very important because "light and bright" helps sell houses, and for more money. This means optimizing the sources and availability of light throughout the interior. This can be achieved in a combination of two ways: natural lighting and electric.

Bring in more natural light

There are two ways to get as much natural light as possible into the home: windows and skylights. Additionally, doors can be included in the window category; many have glass in them and act as additional windows. In my own home, for example, I had a three-quarter-length sheet of glass inserted into the frame of the door. It provides plenty of light to a formerly dark hallway leading to my family room, while still maintaining a sense of privacy because it is completely frosted except for a one-inch clear band around the edge. There is no set rule as to whether you use windows, skylights, or both, or in what proportion, just as long as whatever you do provides the most light possible to the interior of the structure within the structural limitations of the building.

Windows

When adding or changing windows, two things must be considered: size and style. The variety of window styles today is near mind boggling. Used in any individual style—or, based on the needs and configuration of a room, in a combination of styles—they can vastly improve the appearance of a home and add large amounts of light to the interior. Styles include casement, swing-out, fixed, picture, and clerestory.

As far as size of the windows goes, you can basically have almost anything you need or want. Use as much glass as you reasonably can, consistent with the overall size of the room that the window is going into and the direction that the particular room or wall faces.

In certain circumstances, you may want to take advantage of the many different types of glass available in today's window systems. You'll find everything from clear to rippled to frosted. Perhaps, for instance, in a bathroom you want to increase the amount of light coming in, but don't want to sacrifice a potential buyer's sense of privacy. A large window with glass that's either partially or fully frosted addresses both concerns.

As with everything, use caution when upgrading windows. Check out current codes—the windows not only have to match code requirements regarding material and structure, but also, in some cases, for emergency egress. Let's say you want to put a nicer window in a bedroom, but do not want to change the size of the opening. The new codes say that the windows have to be large to permit emergency egress, so now you are stuck not only

Moneysaver

Using windows and skylights to let in natural light saves money because you use less electricity to light the house in all but the night hours.

with replacing the window, but also changing the size of the opening. This will add extra expense to the change that wasn't in your budget.

In choosing your windows, there are two additional considerations:

- Have at least one window in each room wide enough to escape through in case of fire or other emergency.
- Always use double-paned glass. It's great for insulation, helping maintain coolness in the summer and warmth in the winter. In areas of extreme winter cold, consider triple-paned glass.

Both of these concerns, safety and environmental, are commonly found in today's building codes. Check yours to be sure.

Doors

Just as in the case of windows, there is virtually no end to the number of different styles and types of doors you can use to accomplish the goal of adding more light to the home. These include a glass panel in a single door, sliding glass doors, French doors, or the addition of what are called side lights to a doorway. Despite the name, these are not lights, but rather a set of narrow windows that frame the door and let light flood the area surrounding the door.

Even the materials and hardware offer a wide variety. You can have wood or aluminum frames, vertical or horizontal locking systems, and handle or no-handle styles. All of this variety just gives you further opportunity to inexpensively redo a house and still have some uniqueness of design detail.

Skylights

Skylights are another way to increase the amount of natural light coming into the structure. They provide an additional source of light beyond what windows do, and are a good addition when wall size or location limits what you can achieve with window additions.

Skylights are available in a large number of sizes, designs, and materials. The most common for residential use is heavy plastic enclosed in a metal frame. Some are fixed and others can be opened, manually or mechanically, from inside the house. You can also find skylights in flat glass held in heavy metal frames.

Another option for adding a skylight when the overall structure of the building precludes direct access from the room to the roof is a "tube" skylight. As the name suggests, this involves the use of a long cylindrical tube that can be straight or multi-angled connecting glass or plastic "lenses" at either end of the tube. The tube passes through such intermediary areas as an attic or crawl space that separates the ceiling of the involved room from the underside of the roof. Not dissimilar from a periscope, this allows the light to enter through the roof-mounted "lens," descend through the tube, and exit below into the room where the terminal "lens" is located. Tube skylights are much smaller than traditional skylights, and do not provide as much light as a full skylight, but they are a wonderful option

 Watch Out!

Because you are cutting into the solid roof surface to install a skylight, you are breaching the roof's ability to keep out rain and snow. In order to not create a leak at the same time you are increasing the amount of light for the interior, be very careful in your flashing of the outside of the skylight. Properly flashing the skylight is not difficult, but it is an area that, if not done carefully, can cause all kinds of aggravation in terms of leaks once the weather changes.

when you want a skylight in a room or area in which the ceiling
is not directly at roof level.

Add light fixtures

The other way to improve light in a home is the use, both
through placement and number, of electric lighting fixtures. As
with windows, there is no limit to the number of variations in
style and design that is available today in lighting fixtures. You
can run the gamut from heavy-looking industrial hanging fixtures consisting of a plain enameled sloping metal shade and a
single exposed bulb to wall sconces to absolutely dazzling chan-
deliers and stationary central ceiling fixtures. Styles also cover a
huge range, from ultramodern to various "period" fixtures to
utilitarian. There are even styles that incorporate revolving ceiling fans like something out of *Casablanca*. Materials similarly
seem to offer limitless choices. There are fixtures made of
metal, plastic, cloth, paper, and ceramic, as well as multiple
combinations of two or more of these substances.

Not only can you take advantage of a wide spectrum of fixtures for your project, you can also vary the intensity of light
they provide. This is accomplished through the different types
and wattage of bulbs that the various fixtures are made to
accommodate.

In the same vein, the intensity of light can be controlled
when installing the switches. While single switches are the most
common and provide light when flipped on, the use of a rheo-
stat or dimmer switch gives you the ability to choose exactly how
much light you want in an area, depending on the mood you
want to achieve. In areas that will have varied uses, dimmers are
really worth the extra amount you'll spend on them because
you can increase or decrease the amount of light according to
what's going on at a particular moment.

For example, if you're sitting in the living room during the
evening and relaxing with the latest novel, you may want lots of
bright light. Alternatively, perhaps you're hosting a cocktail

Watch Out!

In cosmetic flips where you are trying to limit your expenses, remember that if you decide to not only replace existing fixtures but also add others in new locations, you'll incur the additional expense of having an electrician run new wire to the new location, as well as cutting and repairing the sheetrock where the new fixture is to be placed.

party and would prefer "atmosphere." Just a quick adjustment on the dimmer switch and you've accomplished the change without sacrificing the overall need to have as much light available as might ever be necessary.

Similarly, a combination of different types of lighting fixtures can provide the occupant of the home with a broader choice of amount of lighting in a given room while still allowing maximum potential light for that same room. A good example of this would be combining a centrally mounted ceiling fixture with a number of strategically placed wall sconces, and adding in the combination of multiple switches—perhaps one switch for the ceiling light, and one or more for the wall sconces, depending on the number and location of the sconces.

Tile and stone

Another area where you can vastly improve the appearance of a home with a relatively minimal expenditure of funds is the use of tile and stone. There are four primary places in the typical home where a combination of these materials would provide the greatest benefit. These are the kitchen, bath, fireplace/hearth, and the exterior of the home.

Kitchen and bath

I'll address the kitchen and bath areas together because these usually have commonalities in the types of material and their use. In these areas, both tile and stone find a number of uses. The materials are used in the same ways in each, although to some extent, for different reasons. Counters in both the bathrooms and kitchen can be surfaced in either tile or stone, and sometimes in a combination of the materials. The reasons are the same: appearance, resistance to water, and ease of cleaning. There are two things that determine which, as well as how much, of the materials will be used in a given project: cost and appearance. The cost of stone is generally higher than the cost of ceramic tile, but even with stone, there are ways to utilize the stone and minimize the amount of cost increase over tile that its use incurs.

With ceramic tile, your choices are mainly color, texture, and tile size. Which way you go on any of these is strictly up to you and whatever seems to be most in demand in your local market at the time you do your flip. The wide variety of color available allows you to have the tile contrast or complement the color scheme in your bath or kitchen. You have an additional source of adding color accents to your cosmetics here. This is in the grout you use around the tile once it has been set in the mastic. The grout color can carry the tile color, albeit in a different texture than the tile, or it can be a contrasting accent color.

As far as surface texture is concerned, most ceramic tile has a smooth surface, although there is some that is a little rougher than others. This difference in texture can be deliberate or can be faults in the manufacture of a particular batch of tile. Such production defects do not lessen the tile's ability to repel water, and may make them useful as random accent tiles to the overall smooth surface you install. As an example of this, a bathroom shower stall I once did has a very even color and surface texture, save for the occasional "seconds" I sought out at the tile company specifically to use as accents in the shower enclosure walls.

If you're willing to spend more money in your baths or kitchen, you can do the counters and shower stalls in granite or marble. This is a slightly different process than tile. First, the

Moneysaver

For cosmetic flips, good slab granite or marble can be bought, cut, and installed from Home Depot for less than a fabricator's cost.

selection process is different, and then the installation is different and may have an additional step involved once it is installed.

If you decide to go with granite or marble, there are two ways to do so: slab and tile. In the former case, you pick out long, pre-cut slabs of the stone you want to use. These are usually accessible for consideration at dealers' yards and warehouses where you go from stack to stack of the slabs, examining each slab or group of slabs you wish to consider. The slabs, usually each four by eight feet in size, are then taped with your name and held for your stone fabricator to come by and examine for any hidden defects in the stone that could cause it to break up during fabrication to your project's specifications. Assuming your choice is structurally sound, the stone fabricator picks up the slabs, works them into the finished form and size you require, and then installs them in the home you're flipping. His or her work includes any cutouts that may be necessary for faucets, sinks, stovetops, and spigots included in your design.

Picking out the stone you want is a very interesting process. It is not simply choosing a color the way you might choose ceramic tile. Instead, because no two pieces of granite or marble are ever exactly the same in terms of color or pattern, even when they are the same type of stone, you should carefully look at as many different types that generally match or reasonably contrast with the color scheme you plan to use. Then, based on the natural patterns of internal stone color variations and veins running through the stone, decide on the type of stone and specific slabs you want. The larger the area is that you plan to cover with the particular stone, the more chance for variations in the color and pattern of the stone.

Moneysaver

Granite or marble tile provides the expensive look of these stones but at a dramatically lower cost.

There is one important thing to remember about granite or marble. It is expensive—much more so than ceramic tile. One of the reasons to be doing a cosmetic flip is to maximize your profit with a minimum of expense. So slab granite or marble might be something you'll want to leave aside for now, saving it until you do an intermediate or total gut flip. However, there is a way to use granite or marble and limit the higher costs of that material over ceramic tile. That is to use tile made of the stone. Most good stone dealers not only have a wide selection of slab; they also have a fairly good selection of granite and marble tile. While still being a higher cost item than ceramic tile, it is far cheaper than slab, and provides the same interesting mix of colors and patterns.

In terms of specific characteristics of granite and marble, generally, granite is a harder stone. Because of this, it'll stand up to more abuse on a daily basis. Marble, on the other hand, is usually more porous than granite. This means that it can get stained when some liquids are spilled on it. So it must be sealed when installed, and the sealing must periodically be redone. Both granite and marble have a wide variety of colors and patterns. So your desires in this area should be fairly easy to accommodate.

Fireplace and hearth

The other area inside the home where tile or stone is used is around the fireplace. Ceramic tile is used in far fewer situations than either stone or the traditional brick, both of which are more durable.

Most people are familiar with traditional brick in this area, so I won't say much about it. Stone, however, is coming more into its own in recent years. While fieldstone has, like brick, been in use in the fireplace area for generations, slate and granite are more and more frequently being seen as a stone of choice due to their ranges of color, surface texture, and pattern. Granite in both slab and tile form is often used, as is the rougher-surfaced slate. Often the color of the granite is chosen to match that in the kitchen when the fireplace is in an immediately adjoining room such as a family room. This is done to carry the design and color scheme through more of the house.

As far as the cost is concerned, you can use this stone in the fireplace area and still take advantage of the relative savings found in tile made from the stone, just as I discussed in regards to the kitchen or bathrooms. As with every item, however, the use of a slightly higher expense item over a cheaper one is a decision to be made as you lay out your budget and relate it to the local market you are hoping to serve with your flip.

Curb appeal

Another way to inexpensively improve cosmetic flips is to upgrade the exterior appearance. I'm talking about curb appeal, that look that makes prospective buyers say, "Wow, I've just got to get into that house!" Because this is a cosmetic flip, don't get deeply involved in a total landscaping makeover. Just adding some nice shrubs, including some that are flowering, will achieve a pulled-together look. For a bit more money, you may want to consider replacing the lawn with new sod if the old one's looking really ratty. If not, leave it alone.

As for trees, these can be added, but you're now getting into what can be potentially expensive. Decent-sized trees cost money, and small saplings don't really have much first impression impact even though in a few years they'll look great. (For more detailed information about these aspects of curb appeal, see Chapter 14.)

Curb appeal needn't be just shrubs and trees, however. The careful use of stone can just as impressively enhance the appearance of the house. A front walkway made of Arizona flagstone, for example, can look far more inviting than generic concrete. Perhaps a few pieces of flagstone surrounded by peat or grass will be all that you need. If you choose this approach, however, like everything else, stay with the cheaper grades of stone. Leave the expensive stuff such as Connecticut Bluestone to the higher-end gut projects.

Just the facts

- Be sure to determine what permits are necessary for the project and obtain them before getting started.

- There are many different materials sources—check out more than one and you will likely save some money.

- A single color of paint can save money over multiple colors. Be sure to use the type of paint best suited to the room where it's going.

- Cabinets can be made to look brand new by refacing and changing the hardware.

- Combining natural and electric lighting can have a very dramatic and positive effect on the house and its appearance to buyers.

- Don't forget curb appeal—small, inexpensive touches such as planting some shrubs or enhancing the walkway can make a big impact.

GET THE SCOOP ON...
Changing or upgrading the kitchen ▪ Making
improvements to the bathroom ▪ Living room
options ▪ "Going light" on the rest of the house

Intermediate Flips

Chapter 11

L et's look at your options when you are willing to spend a bit more on your project and become more deeply involved in it. An intermediate flip is a good way to prepare yourself for ultimately doing full makeovers—total guts, which I'll discuss in the next chapter. This is because an intermediate flip requires a lot more planning, a larger budget, and a great deal more time and effort to successfully complete than a cosmetic flip. It is also a limited version of the type of involvement required in a total gut.

In doing an intermediate flip, you concentrate on a portion of the house as the area or areas where you'll do a lot of major work and "cosmeticize" the rest of the house so that the finished product looks totally redone. Nothing could be worse than finishing an intermediate flip to have the redone kitchen and baths look like they came from the pages of *Architectural Digest*, while the balance of the house remains a throwback to the immediate post-World War II construction that it began as. You don't want people saying, "Okay, so you redid the kitchen."

What you *do* want is, "Wow, this whole house is fabulous! The remodel is absolutely amazing."

If there is a general rule of thumb in determining where you should put the most effort, it is "Spend for your highest likely return." In most cases, this means the kitchen, bathrooms, and family room or great room. True, there will be cases where some other part of a home brings a better return, but those cases are due to the unique characteristics of the home in question. The broader part of the home-buying public usually concentrates importance in kitchens, baths, and family gathering areas before others.

Kitchens

Whereas I discussed kitchens and baths together in Chapter 10, I'll address them separately both here and in Chapter 12. The reason for this is simple. In cosmetic flips, we were, for the most part, just making surface changes—a little paint or wallpaper, perhaps refacing cabinets, and maybe some new tile—and we were done. In intermediate flips, we're going way beyond that in at least some of the property we're working on.

In the kitchen of an intermediate flip, the most common areas to consider changing or upgrading are:

- Countertops
- Cabinets
- Appliances
- Sinks and fixtures
- Vents
- Floors (in some cases)

You might also use paint or wallpaper on the walls for the "frosting-on-the-cake" effect it will add to the heavy work you'll be doing here, but the focus in the kitchen is on replacing, not refacing.

Countertops

The first thing to do with the countertops is to tear out the old ones. Depending on the planned design of the finished kitchen, you may be using the same counter layout, adding to it, or replacing some of it with a center island design. Whatever the design, do the countertops from scratch. As in the case of the cosmetic flip, counters can be covered in ceramic tile or stone, the latter being either slab or tile. I thoroughly discussed the differences, pro and con, in Chapter 10, so I won't get too deeply into that subject here, other than to note that you may wish to use the more expensive choice if the market you're in expects granite as opposed to ceramic tile. If you are in such a market, the extra expense will likely be rewarded with a higher sale price when you bring your finished product to market.

Although I won't be going over the basics of tile and stone again, there are a couple of other choices that you have for countertops in kitchens where you're spending more money: concrete and acrylic.

Concrete countertops

Concrete is basically the same stuff you find on your front sidewalk. However, over the last few years it has taken quite a few steps up the design ladder by virtue of creative individuals perfecting the methods used to custom shape and color it for uses other than those more common traditional ones.

As used in kitchen counters, concrete has the same qualities of hardness and durability, but it has become much more a design feature of higher-end kitchens. Unlike slab, which is custom cut to the size of your counter needs, concrete is custom molded or poured to meet your dimensions. During the fabrication process,

 Moneysaver

If you are adding stone countertops, use tiles rather than the slab form of the stone. Doing so can cut your costs by as much as two thirds.

it also has color added if you decide that basic concrete gray isn't what you want in your kitchen. Although the coloration is more of a tint than a loud solid color, it can be blended into the overall color scheme of your kitchen to accent or contrast with your chosen color. Once installed, the counter surface is then sealed to prevent juices or other liquids from seeping into the surface pores of the concrete. However, in a few cases, the sealing fails to work completely, so keep that in mind as a possible source of problems down the road with your ultimate buyer.

In terms of its adaptability to a particular plan or counter design, concrete is as adaptable as anything available. This is because it's poured to be used in the plans you are working from. Whether your kitchen is a galley style, has a built-in breakfast nook, or has a center island, concrete is very workable for your situation. It can be more expensive than the same amount of stone, due to the custom pouring and coloring/fabrication involved. However, in upscale homes, it is definitely an option worth looking into.

Acrylic countertops

Acrylic has many characteristics that make it another good option for your counters. In addition to all of the features that exist with slab stone, as well as concrete, acrylic can be more highly colored. This provides you with an even larger set of options in the choice of your color scheme and the method with which you apply it. Acrylic is also very strong and durable, so you can cut on it or pound whatever foods call for pounding without worrying about damaging the counter. The material itself is a chemically created substance that has previously been used in a wide variety of situations and industries. It has only recently come to be used in home construction. While Corian, which is also an acrylic, has been around for 30 years, the type of acrylic I refer to is custom molded and colored for your project. As with concrete, it is a more expensive option, but well worth considering for upscale homes.

Cabinets

If you're doing an intermediate flip, you could reface the cabinets as discussed in Chapter 10, or you could tear out all the old cabinets and replace them with brand-new ones. Which choice you make depends in large part on the market you are going to be selling into and the basic structural condition of the existing cabinets. Additionally, you may very well be changing the floor plan of the kitchen in your intermediate flip, whereas you work with the existing plan in a cosmetic flip. If a change in the layout of the kitchen is part of your plan, the choice has already been made—you'll install new cabinets.

As with everything else, there is a wide range of prices for new cabinets. On the less expensive end, you can get a good selection of cabinet styles, sizes, and materials from large home improvement stores such as Home Depot. There are also kitchen design stores that can provide you with pre-manufactured "basic" design cabinets. There is absolutely nothing wrong with either of these routes, and they are found in homes at almost all price levels. You order them, they are delivered, and you install them, adding the appropriate hardware after you have done so. The different styles available are fairly broad, so you can pretty much handle almost any kitchen design you have in mind for your flip.

At the other end of the spectrum are custom cabinets. For these, the price is whatever you're willing to pay, based on the design and type of wood used. The point to remember is that, for a start, the cabinets are custom designed and built specifically for your kitchen, which makes them more expensive. However, if you stick with common woods such as oak or birch,

 Moneysaver

Save time and money by installing pre-manufactured cabinets purchased from a large home improvement store.

most of the extra cost will be in the custom design work. But you can get as exotic as you want in your choice of wood.

For example, let's say you want maple cabinets. Maple has a nice, light color, is a hardwood, and has good durability. Now you have to decide whether the maple you want is clear maple, bird's-eye maple, or fiddleback maple. The latter two are more expensive than the basic maple you thought you wanted when you chose maple. This is because each of them has a unique grain not found in basic maple. Bird's-eye maple and fiddleback maple are much scarcer and therefore more expensive.

Maybe you want something a bit more interesting. Perhaps, after viewing sample chips of wood, you decide that you like northern white ash or, better yet, ironwood. Both have beautiful grains and an almost luminous glow. They also have a very high price. You can go through this process on almost any type of wood, but I think you get the picture. If you are flipping a very high-end house in a very high-end market, the extra expense is definitely justified. In such a situation, the market will likely pay the higher price you'll charge for the finished flip, and you have correctly chosen the higher-end wood. I have seen Brazilian cherry cabinets and mahogany cabinets in situations such as these. Just keep in mind that you have a goal—making a profit—and you must follow the budget you've assembled as closely as possible.

Aside from the cost considerations, there are other similarities and differences to consider when weighing custom cabinets against manufactured cabinets:

- Manufactured cabinets tend to be less expensive unless you use the more expensive brands.

- Manufactured cabinets often have harder and more durable surfaces.

- Manufactured cabinets often have more unique types of features than custom cabinets, such as specialty pull outs.

- Custom cabinets can be made to exact sizes, eliminating the need for filler pieces.

Watch Out!

The more unique the wood, the more you'll pay. Presumably, if you're considering custom cabinetry, you've already accounted for it in the budget. If not, stop and think it over carefully before upgrading out of your budget.

Once you decide on the type of cabinet, you will have to select your hardware—handles, pulls, and hinges (see Chapter 10).

Appliances

The next things to consider in your new kitchen are the appliances. Prices range from the inexpensive, basic range, refrigerator, or dishwasher to the most expensive stove made by Thermador or Wolf, dishwasher offered by Miele or Bosch, or refrigerator by Sub Zero. Your choice depends on two considerations: kitchen plans and market. Clearly, you must select appliances that coordinate with the design of the kitchen you're doing based on your budget and plans. It does little good to have a massive commercial-grade Wolf range in a kitchen in which cabinet space is at a premium and there's no room for a vent/fan. Likewise, it will do you little good when you come to market if the flip is in a neighborhood of high-end homes and all you have to offer are appliances from the bottom of the price range—a tiny refrigerator and a single-cycle dishwasher in basic white enamel.

In addition to the quality of the appliances, consider the finish of the units. Do you want enamel, stainless, or custom front panel? Each of these options has its own price range and fits a particular customer market. Additionally, the appliance finish is adaptable to the overall style and design of the kitchen it's going to be part of.

If you're doing a flip in a middle-income neighborhood and concentrating on color in your kitchen, you may be able to have the front panels and doors of the appliances match or complement that color scheme. On the other hand, if you're in a higher-end project, you may desire to go with all-stainless, or, alternatively, with a front panel on each appliance made of the same wood that the cabinets are made of. Some of the better brands have wood-front panels available that are so well matched that, at first glance, one doesn't immediately see a demarcation between cabinets and appliances. However, the way to have an even better match is to have the firm doing your custom cabinets provide the front appliance panels. Then the match is perfect.

In both an intermediate flip and a total gut, there are other types of appliances to consider that normally would never find their way into a simple cosmetic flip. Whether you include any or all of these depends on the overall structural plans and the market at which you're directing the flip, as well as the budget you've set. Such additional appliances include:

- **Wine coolers.** These small, refrigerator-like units have racks specially designed to hold individual bottles of wine, five or six to a rack, at a temperature that is best for chilling wine without ruining it. They usually come with a glass-paneled door, so you can tell at a glance what you've got on chill without having to open the door.

- **Wet bar refrigerators.** These small mini-fridges built in under a wet bar enable you to keep ice, chilled mixers, and anything else a well-stocked bar might require while entertaining.

- **Deep freezers.** A deep freezer is a place where larger amounts of food can be kept frozen until the owner decides to take something out and cook it. Usually full-sized freezer units are not placed in the kitchen but in out-of-the-way locations such as garages, basements, or utility rooms. However, a smaller freezer unit capable of storing a couple of weeks' worth of food can be worked into a larger kitchen very conveniently.

- **Bun warmers.** These simple metal drawers, usually stainless steel-fronted, are built into the front of a counter and are used to warm trays of buns or a loaf or two of bread just before serving.

■ **Built-in countertop blender units.** Countertop blenders, which frequently double as ice crushers, are just like any blender you might find in a kitchen, except for one important difference. They do not have a movable base taking up space on the counter. Instead, the base mechanism is permanently built into the counter with a flat cover protecting it until use. The glass portion of the blender, as well as its blades and cover, separates and stores in a cabinet or drawer until use.

Sinks and fixtures

No kitchen, from world-class to basic bottom-of-the-budget, can operate without a sink. In a kitchen of the type you'll be doing for either an intermediate or total gut, you'll be more likely to spend more on a sink. This also allows you a greater number of choices. You have to decide if you want a larger single sink or smaller side-by-side double sinks. The total size of the sink here is the same; it's just that each individual divided section is smaller.

Sink materials can vary widely. Today, two of the more common materials in kitchen sinks, regardless of type or design, are stainless steel or unpolished stone. Of the two, stainless is the more common. The unpolished stone is usually found only in the much higher-end homes, as it's quite a bit more costly than stainless. Besides these two materials, in more basic designed kitchens, the material may be enameled cast iron. In this case, the color is usually white, but can be had in something else to blend with the overall color scheme of the kitchen.

When the design is chosen based on the wishes of the ultimate owner, either of the options, single sink or double, is used. However, as you are building this to flip, the choice is entirely yours. Some folks wouldn't think of having a kitchen without two separate side-by-side sinks so they can wash vegetables in one, while simultaneously cleaning up dirty pots in the other.

Bright Idea

Consider including a "ready-hot" faucet, which instantly provides hot water for making hot tea, coffee, or a bowl of soup. Increasingly, such faucet devices are being combined with the capability of providing filtered cold water for drinking by using a separate handle or switch from the one controlling the hot liquid.

Conversely, and I happen to be one of these, there are people who want nothing to do with double sinks. They prefer to have one large sink and use it for various tasks. It's a matter of personal taste. Neither is "right" or "wrong."

Sink fixtures are likely to be more plentiful and possibly more expensive in both the intermediate and total gut kitchen than in a cosmetic, although at some basic level this will be your choice. The best fixtures—and there are figuratively as many to choose from as there are trees in a small forest—can either have separate faucets for hot and cold water, or a single faucet that combines the two functions into one unit. You should also have a spray hose unit for cleanup of the sink area as well as for washing vegetables, and a garbage disposal unit that won't choke on the first heavy load of lettuce leaves your buyer flushes down the drain.

The spray hose can be a separate unit mounted at the edge of the sink that retracts beneath counter level when not in use or a retractable extension of the faucet/spigot unit if you go single-faucet style. In the latter case, the unit stays enclosed in the cylinder that is the spigot housing and acts as a normal spigot. When the user wants spray action he or she merely pulls the end of the spigot forward out of the sleeve and presses a switch or other device on the top of it. There are many models on the market. My favorite manufacturer is the German firm, Grohe.

Vents

The vent is used to eliminate the odors and smoke from cooking on the stovetop as much as possible. There are two ways to handle the vent requirements of the modern kitchen. Which you use depends largely on the overall design of the kitchen and where the stove is positioned within that design.

If you have a free-standing range type of stove, it is likely that you'll use a ceiling-mounted vent. If, on the other hand, your cooking surface is an island-mounted stovetop, it is more likely that your vent will be a retractable one built into the rear of the counter behind the stovetop or the stovetop itself. It rises, usually to a height of about 6 inches, and descends by the push of a button mounted alongside the stovetop.

While it is feasible to have a ceiling-mounted vent over an island-mounted stovetop, this is usually the least preferred format as it hovers over the center of everything and gives the impression of overwhelming everything around it. However, it is again a matter of personal choice. I had a client insist on a ceiling-mounted vent when the cooking surface was a good 10 feet from the nearest wall. She solved the problem by having the vent chimney, the part where the exhaust rises to exit through the roof outlet, custom made over 5 feet in length. However, a solution like this is expensive, and, again, will affect your bottom line.

Vents do more than just remove smoke and odors from the cooking area. Most of today's ceiling-mounted vent hoods also have built-in lighting with a variety of intensities, and come with a choice of intensity of exhaust fan or fans, depending on the amount and heaviness of the odors produced by the particular meal being created. As if all of this weren't enough, many vents also have built-in warming lights and plate racks or spice shelves, or a combination of all of these items.

Floors

In a kitchen, the choice of material used for flooring is very important, and not only due to appearance. The typical heavy use of a kitchen area requires that something that has durability along with its appearance be used. Although there are a few folks who think you can have carpet in a kitchen, my advice is, "Don't!" In a kitchen, you have constant heavy traffic, in addition to the likelihood of spills of water, grease, food, and garbage. If your kitchen layout also has an eating area, whether at a center island or in an adjoining breakfast nook, you have the additional wear and tear of chairs being moved in and out across the floor to consider.

These factors almost certainly mandate your use of one of three materials, or a combination of them. These are wood (including bamboo), stone, or tile (ceramic or synthetic). All provide a nice appearance and will work with virtually any design plans you may have on a particular project. If you decide to go with wood, the type of wood is, as with everything else, a matter of choice. However, hardwood lasts longer than soft, and it appears that the newest addition to the "wood" market, bamboo, lasts even longer than hardwood. However, if you use wood, make sure that it's not soft wood. The kitchen is a high-traffic area, and only a good hardwood (including bamboo) will do. I keep specifically mentioning bamboo not to suggest that you necessarily use it, but just to note that it is very durable, and increasingly being used where, formerly, hardwood was the likely choice.

If you decide to use wood, it doesn't have to be the same as your cabinets. You can do so, but there is no requirement to do so. My own kitchen has custom maple cabinets and I have oak floors with a light stain on them for color. However, whichever type you use, you should have a good heavy varnish laid down over it to protect the wood itself from the spills and traffic combination it is going to have to endure. In essence, you should have it sealed against any of the very predictable spills that will occur. Also, because of their proximity to each other, the wood you choose for flooring should probably be the same that you use in the great room that often is contiguous with the kitchen.

 Watch Out!

Kitchen floors must be able to withstand high traffic and all kinds of spills. Choose your material with that in mind.

Bright Idea

Increase the design appeal of wood floors by laying a contrasting colored wood border around the outside of the floor where it meets the bottom of the wall. It not only accents the area, it also says "quality" to potential buyers.

I have seen many different types of stone used for kitchen flooring. The most common are some form of slate, such as colored flagstones or Connecticut Bluestone, limestone, and even tumbled Italian marble tiles. All of these are quite a bit more costly than wood or ceramic and synthetic tiles, so again, it depends on your intended market and your budget as much as your preference. One of the most expensive kitchen floors I ever saw in a flip had one-foot squares of milled French limestone, which extended out to the adjoining breakfast room. It was a beautiful floor and went perfectly with the kitchen, but it was for a very high-end market.

If you decide to go with tile, your choices are either some form of ceramic tile or some type of factory-manufactured synthetic tile. In either case, you have a wide variety of colors and designs from which to choose, so finding something that goes with your intended design should not be a problem. You can have virtually every color or pattern under the sun in synthetic tile, and even find a number of products that imitate the look of brick or stone in a synthetic. Ceramics, on the other hand, offer a broad choice of everything from 12-inch-square Mexican-style pavers to geometric-patterned flat tile that can be accented by the color of the grouting between the individual tiles.

Once you decide on the type of floor material you plan to use, you can further increase the uniqueness of design in the area by accenting it with borders or dividers inlaid in the floor of contrasting strips of wood, or of a different colored or sized tile. For example, perhaps you elect to use 12-inch Mexican pavers for your kitchen floor, but you would like to brighten up the basic terra cotta color with some accent color. Every five or six feet, you can insert a brightly colored or patterned tile as an accent piece for the floor. The color of this accent tile can match the color you plan to paint the walls, or it can be something totally different, something solely for its accent effect. You might similarly have your color accent tile laid in a running strip around the border of the floor.

Bathroom

In redoing a bathroom or bathrooms, you run into many of the same considerations that you confronted in the kitchen: counters and cabinets. Your choices in material and design are, for the most part, very similar. You may keep the same type of wood and finish as in the kitchen, vary it in all baths, or match one to the kitchen and vary other baths as you see fit and as the local dominant custom dictates. You also have the same options available to you in the hardware for the cabinets and drawers.

Bathroom sinks definitely veer away from the kitchen models. There are a wide variety of styles and designs on the market today. These cover the range from metal to porcelain, to ceramic basin to glass—yes, I said glass—to concrete. There are a number of variations on the shape of the basin. While you can certainly have some form of the traditional round basin, there are square or rectangular basins that slope very gradually from the front edge toward the rear and the drain that is placed there.

Separate from these items, there are certain considerations that are unique to bathrooms. These include what type of tub and shower fixture you will use, the type of tub, and the material in the surrounding enclosure. Today, it can be tile, stone, or concrete. There is even acrylic, but is very expensive, so you would not be likely to use it unless you were doing a very high-end flip.

Additionally, there is the question of what to use for a shower enclosure. Will you leave it open and protect against shower spray with a simple shower curtain, or will you have glass, either in the form of sliding panels or in a glass door and adjoining wall? Shower curtains are much less expensive than

Watch Out!

Due to the moisture found in bathrooms, don't use wood flooring there.

glass surrounds or shower doors, and come in a wide variety of styles to suit any décor.

For flooring, you will want to use something that is impervious to water, such as ceramic tile, stone, or other manmade surface. Also, because of moisture concerns, you should have a vent in the bathroom, preferably with a built-in fan. Opening a window can serve the same purpose, but a vent/fan arrangement is much more efficient, and not that expensive.

Family/great room

The family room, sometimes referred to as the "great room," is a concept that has existed in many American homes for decades. In recent years, it has made a dramatic comeback in popularity. Usually adjoining the kitchen, it has become not just a family gathering place, but also a combination party location and entertainment center for family and guests.

Due to its location and uses, the finishing of the room should follow the details of the kitchen. This usually means that whatever type of flooring material you use, whatever color paint or paper you use on the walls, you will continue it through the family room. This continuity even extends to the type of cabinetry you decide upon. Although functionality differs from kitchen to great room, the design, pulls, and handles, as well as the material they are made of, will remain the same as in the kitchen. There are a couple of reasons for this. First, it ensures that design-wise the two rooms complement each other, rather than clash. Second, it gives the visual effect of extending the size of each of the two rooms, so that it seems that there is a much larger space in the area than there actually is.

As far as the particular types of cabinets are concerned, the family room cabinets will likely be more of a combination of drawers and cabinets to hold items such as CDs, DVDs, photo collections, and games, alongside open shelves for the stereo system components, books, photos, and collectibles. You might even have the sound system component spaces built in or hidden in individual cabinets to provide a more uncluttered look.

"Going light"

At this point, we have looked at the most likely areas of a house to receive the heaviest attention and resources in the typical intermediate flip. But what about the rest of the house? In most cases, the balance of the structure will be treated in much the same way as your cosmetic flip. Remember, the two most important things in an intermediate flip are:

- Concentrating funds and materials for complete makeovers in a few individual parts of the house that will most likely bring the highest return on your overall investment

- At the same time, making sure that the whole house is attractive and appealing to potential buyers

That is why it is an intermediate flip. It is more or less equidistant between cosmetic flips and total guts.

So, what do you do for the rest of the house? Go light. Treat it as you would an entire house on which you're only doing a cosmetic flip. Pick out attractive paints and/or wallpapers in good combinations and apply them in the most decorative manner that will appeal to the largest portion of the home-buying marketplace. Do the same with such items as windows and window coverings, as well as trim and moldings. Also, where a change in a few lighting fixtures in key locations will improve the appearance and appeal, make the change.

Remember, too, that just as in a cosmetic flip, curb appeal is important. Be certain that the sidewalks, gates, driveway, and fences have an appealing appearance. A few strategically placed inexpensive flowers and shrubs will complete the picture. As an added attraction to buyers, you may find it a good idea to invest in a basic drip irrigation and sprinkler system with an automatic timer. For the added cost of as little as a few hundred dollars you have an added selling feature, and at the same time have reduced the worry of having the lawn or gardens die for lack of watering just as you go on market.

Now you're ready to bring your intermediate flip to market.

Just the facts

- In an intermediate flip, concentrate the heavy money on the most profitable return areas: kitchen and baths.

- Maintain continuity in the kitchen and great room areas by using the same flooring materials and cabinetry.

- It is important to remember that bathrooms have location-specific moisture issues that must be dealt with in your construction.

- The balance of the house should be treated in much the same way that you would in a basic cosmetic flip. Make it look good, but keep the expensive work confined to the kitchen and baths.

GET THE SCOOP ON...
Understanding permits and entitlements ▪ The
impact of local regulations on your project ▪
Electrical, plumbing, and structural construction
issues ▪ Interior design details ▪ Adding an exterior structure ▪ Recreational "extras"

Total Gut and Remodels

Chapter 12

Well, we've finally made the complete trek
from the easiest of flips to the true heavy
lifting. In this chapter I discuss the most
involved and costliest type of flip—the total gut. It's
the ultimate flip, where you basically take apart the
entire house and rebuild it, sometimes from the
foundation up, and sometimes a little shy of that
extreme, perhaps merely gutting the entire structure
inside the four walls and rebuilding it. You may find
yourself adding a wing or an extra room(s), or you
may be satisfied in your overall planning and work to
settle for a total rearrangement of the floor plan.

There will be some of the same concerns in a
total gut that you faced in the other two types of flips
(see Chapters 10 and 11), but there will also be many
more and they will be more encompassing than with
either of the other two types. In short, I break them
down into the following areas:

- Permits and entitlements
- Local regulations

- Construction issues, such as electrical, plumbing, and structural

- Interior design details, such as extra stories, rooms, or wings

- External additions, such as patios, decks, driveways, or fences

- Recreational extras, such as pools, tennis courts, or putting greens

Permits and entitlements

I discussed this area in Chapter 10; however, I will go into more detail here because you're going to be spending far more time and money on such items in a total gut than you have on any of the previous flips.

Permits and entitlements are, for the most part, synonymous, with possibly some differences from locale to locale. Basically, they cover what the governing municipality will or will not allow you to do in the construction of your project. Permits have a couple of purposes, some more legitimate, in my opinion, than others. But whatever the purpose in a particular case, they comprise a necessary step in the process to get your project built and back on the market.

The most obvious reason for permits is that the governing authority that oversees construction in your area uses them to ensure that you are adhering to all zoning, health, and safety codes related to the particular task you are undertaking. Simply put, if your plans for a part of your structure or for one of the operating systems, such as electrical, do not adhere to the requirements spelled out in the codes for that task or system, you will not be given a permit. Without a permit, you cannot legally proceed on your project. That is not to say that any number of projects don't get completed without proper permits. But to proceed in such a manner subjects the builder (you) to all kinds of legal liability, both civil and, in certain extreme cases, criminal. Another facet of completing your project without all

Watch Out!

If authorities discover you went without permits, they can, at best, force you to pay the permit fee and a penalty (sometimes equal to or exceeding the basic fee), or at worst, make you tear out all of the offending unpermitted work. That will definitely put a hole in your projected profit. It is far better to get the permits up front and then follow them to the letter!

the proper permits is that, at least in some locales, it makes it that much more difficult for you to sell your project, particularly for the full price you seek.

A second reason for some permits being required is that it is a way for the local government to generate revenue. Like it or not, in today's world of cash-restricted governments, permits have joined the age-old sources of extra revenue of traffic and parking tickets.

Some types of permitting are a case of submitting your plans along with the proper fee and picking up the appropriate permit. This is frequently the case where the permit sought is for internal systems or installations, such as a new electrical circuit breaker box, a hot water heater, or installation of kitchen or bath counters or cabinets. If the plans comply with applicable code, the permits will usually be approved.

However, when the permit is related to the overall structure, as well as any external part of the process, a whole series of unique challenges frequently come to the fore. There are two that must be addressed immediately. First, you should have considered during your initial planning on the project the issue of how difficult the local planning authority usually makes it to obtain permits for new construction. Some cities and towns have a well-deserved reputation of being as tough as could be imagined on new permit approval. These localities almost always seem to be able to throw up any number of reasons to delay or prevent you from getting your permits and proceeding with your project. Some of these issues are legitimate, such as zoning limits on setbacks and internal living space. Others are overzealous enforcement of the tiniest of details in the local codes. Hopefully, as we discussed in Chapter 7 on planning, you had some lengthy conversations with the local planning and building authorities to try and limit potential objections to your permitting needs. In any event, this is part of the process in order to get started on your actual project once you have the property.

Public hearing

Usually, there will be a review of your plans for the structure of the building by the appropriate officials. In addition, you will frequently find it necessary to submit your plans to a public hearing of some type, be it a design review or planning hearing, where not only the approving authorities have a say as to your permits, but also members of the general public have an opportunity to weigh in with support or opposition to your plans.

At the public hearing, not only your plans and artist's renderings of the finished home will be on view, but frequently samples of outside finishes, paints, shingles, and pavings will be examined before a decision is rendered by the planning group on your permit. When it comes time for the Planning or Building Department to decide on your permit at these hearings, they can either approve, deny, or, adding time to the process, require you to make some changes that you and they agree on, and then come back for a rehearing at some specific time in the future, usually a few weeks or a month.

Consider the neighbors

A second item you should definitely consider is how the neighbors feel about your project. Usually only voiced at the public hearing, the feelings of the neighbors for or against the project have likely been coming together for some time, in some cases since the house you bought for your project originally came on the market. Neighbors may have absolutely no financial stake in your project, but if they are generally opposed to it and start organizing against you, it could end up being worse for you than a visit to hell. On the other hand, if they generally support the project you are putting forward, it will usually mean a much smoother ride to the finish with your permit application.

What I strongly recommend in this case, and a number of my clients religiously do so, is to talk with the neighbors in the project area. Meet with them individually, or more conveniently, in small groups at your office or in their homes and hear what they have to say. In many cases they seek assurance that the new structure is not going to adversely affect the neighborhood or be grossly out of style for the neighborhood. Such meetings and conversations can go a long way toward easing the worries and possible opposition of the neighborhood.

In my own neighborhood, two separate projects recently came up for initial planning commission approval. One was almost unanimously opposed by the neighbors, as well as by an entire spectrum of local civic citizens' bodies. So far, it has not managed to get approvals. The other project was supported by almost 100 percent of those local people speaking at the initial planning hearing, and, while still having a few steps in the process to go, is widely expected to gain its approval.

> **❝**I like having a wine-and-cheese reception at the site, with plans tacked to the walls. The neighbors can come and ask questions. If there is an architect, he or she can also be present to answer questions. Neighbors never like change, and it's not that you will change your plans for them. However, half the battle is that they want to be heard and have their opinions considered.**❞**
>
> —Robert, experienced flipper

There were two main differences between the two projects. One was attempting to insert heavier population and traffic into a quiet residential area that borders a mixed-use area, while the other was designed to fit within its area, and actually improve the surrounding area through its mix of residential and retail space. The other difference was the apparent lack of advance consideration for the feelings and opinions of the surrounding neighbors in the first case, compared to early contacts through mail, phone, and open meetings hosted by the flippers in the other case.

Local regulations

I mentioned that permits are most often concerned with health, safety, and zoning regulations. While the first two seem self-explanatory, the third can be very perplexing. Usually zoning regulations are drawn in order to control or direct the development of a city or neighborhood according to the wishes of the local government, its citizens, or both. Setback rules are an excellent example of this. These specify how far back at a minimum from the boundary of the parcel of land the walls of the house must be placed. It is generally a good regulation, as it precludes "lot line to lot line" construction where one building literally almost touches the next all the way down the street.

Other types of zoning regulations govern mass of the houses, height, and types of structures in a neighborhood. For example, you generally can't build a factory in a neighborhood zoned residential. Sometimes new zoning regulations are instituted in response to a perceived problem that has arisen. Limiting certain types of commercial establishments in their proximity to schools or churches is one example. Another is limiting the size of the living area in proportion to the lot size. Looking into all of these regulations is part of the process you undertake when you discuss permitting issues with your local permitting authority.

In some areas, the simple act of totally razing a house to replace it with a new one, presumably of better construction and design, can trigger zoning rules limiting the construction of the new building—in some cases so severely as to make going forward hardly worthwhile. In these cases, preserving the minimum amount of the original house acceptable to local authorities from the original structure may be enough to maintain the "grandfathered" status of the property and have it apply to your new one. This would save you a large amount of time and money, and, possibly, even the project itself.

Building codes of the health and safety nature are usually enacted either in response to a previous problem or series of problems of a particular nature or to avoid potential dangerous or devastating things from happening in the future. For example, many municipalities now mandate that new construction must include at least double-paned windows. Although more expensive initially, they save a great deal over the life of a structure in the savings in heating and electricity from use of air conditioning. In much colder climes, codes may mandate triple-paned windows. This type of code is not dissimilar in its own way from codes specifying the amount of insulation that must be used in construction of a house. They are based on the same concerns.

From a safety point of view, many local governments now require that circuit breakers be used instead of fuse boxes, as the former cannot be manually overridden by the homeowner as easily when they shut off, and therefore are less likely to allow a resident-created fire hazard. Similarly, the majority of local authorities require ground fault circuit interrupters (GFCIs) be installed in any area where there is an electrical outlet close to a source or use of water. Most common in baths and kitchens, GFCIs reduce the chance of electric shock due to a short circuit in these parts of the home. When a short occurs, they cut off the power to the outlet involved.

These are just a few examples of health- and safety-related codes commonly found in the country today. Others may require specific types of siding or roofing in high fire danger areas, or require extra-high foundations in flood areas, or, in seismically active areas, the addition of shear walls in construction. The point is that wherever you are doing your project, there will be codes that will have to be addressed in your plans in order to get your permits approved.

Bright Idea

Consider a month-to-month lease agreement. Just be certain the tenant fully understands the short-term nature of the arrangement.

All of the planning and permit work takes time, even when your architect has already drawn most of the working drawings at the time immediately following your acquisition of the property. While all of this is going on, the meter is running on your interest owed to the bank with no income coming in to help balance the accounts. Assuming the house on which you're going to do the total gut isn't an uninhabitable wreck, you may want to consider having a short-term tenant rent it from you during the pre-gut period while you're pre-occupied with obtaining permits and the like. It probably won't come close to covering all of your project-related expenses, but it will provide at least a minimal cash flow to help offset some of the ongoing interest expense during this period. Just make certain that if you do rent it out, the lease specifically allows you ongoing reasonable access to the structure during this period so that your planning-related needs are not delayed by a recalcitrant tenant.

Construction issues

In a total gut, one thing you can be certain of is that all of the basic operating systems of the house—plumbing, electrical, structural, heating and air conditioning—will be virtually completely replaced by new systems. It is very likely that the building you're going to gut is an older one with systems that were installed when governing codes and lifestyles were dramatically different. As lifestyles have changed over the years, and the everyday conveniences with them, many different and additional demands have been made on the operating systems of the typical home. While I won't attempt to tell you the exact type of circuit breaker box or kitchen faucet fixtures to use, I will try to point out areas that you should carefully consider in your planning and construction, and where you should work closely with your relevant subcontractor in each of these areas. Almost all of the suggestions I'll make here are based on the commonality of various modern conveniences or lifestyle options that are in demand and have become common in the last few years.

Electrical

The first thing to figure on in your total gut is a larger breaker box. This is because you will probably have more circuits to account for than the old box will handle, and in many areas of the house, you'll have items making heavier demands on electricity than before. While many heating experts favor gas as the least expensive form of home heating, many homes still have electrical heating. While this heating source has been around for decades, the types of electrical heating systems have changed over the years, and they have their own unique demands. On the flip side, before the mid-1950s, air conditioning was virtually non-existent. Then we started with individual window units that plugged into an outlet in the involved room. Now, although window units still exist, central air conditioning is much more common. However, it draws a significant amount of power and requires its own circuit in the overall electrical setup of a home.

Modern kitchens have more use of electricity today than ever before. Even when the cooking appliance is gas, more of the other appliances commonly found in a home today require electricity than ever before. Examples are higher-tech dishwashers, larger refrigerators, wine coolers, microwaves, convection ovens, exhaust fans, blenders, coffee makers, and many other items too numerous to mention here. When you add in the higher-intensity lighting commonly found in today's modern kitchen, you can see the importance of having adequate electrical circuitry in your planning. To cover this issue, codes today often require that many kitchen appliances have their own dedicated circuits, not just sufficient amperage.

As if all of this weren't enough, in family rooms and dens throughout the country, we find a variety of electrical games, sound systems, computers, and televisions that require increasing amounts of electricity to run. Finally, add in the washer and, in many homes, electric dryer, and you can readily see why it is imperative to plan on a total redesign of the electrical system of your project from its previous layout. In fact, in higher-end homes, it is very common to have the entire home wired for sound and computer use no matter where in the house an occupant may be. In fact, it is now common to wire every room for high-speed Internet (CAT-5), cable, and telephone. Some even wire rooms to a central stereo system. For high-end homes, there are even computerized lighting systems where you can set various mood lighting in any room at the push of a button.

Plumbing

The requirements that exist for a more extensive, larger system in a home's electrical system are also found in its plumbing. Whereas the typical single family home built through the 1970s had its basic washer for clothing, a refrigerator, the requisite number of toilets and bathtubs or showers, as well as possibly one or two outdoor faucets for yard use, today's home has gone far beyond this level of plumbing system requirements.

A typical well-appointed home today has all of the expected plumbing systems of older homes, as well as some or all of the following:

- Multiple shower heads in a given shower
- A separate line for instant hot and/or filtered cold water
- A line for the refrigerator's ice-making and filtered drink water dispensing attachments
- A separate wet bar area for use away from the main sink (it's not unusual to find wet bar setups in areas of the home such as the living room, den, family room, master suite, or home office)
- Two dishwashers

- A separate sink, and sometimes a shower, in the garage to allow the home mechanic an opportunity to clean up before coming inside the living area
- For homes with pools or hot tubs, separate bathrooms and/or showers so users can wash off chlorine or suntan oil
- Some form of sprinkler or irrigation system

In an increasing number of communities there is an additional water requirement that is being mandated on a safety basis in new construction on homes. This is the inclusion of an in-home sprinkler system to combat fires. Such a system has to be expertly installed, usually by someone specially trained in such installation, as opposed to a regular plumber, although some plumbers have been trained in such installation and now offer the service as part of their business. The costs of such a system are quite high, but worth it because it helps minimize damage from a fire in the home.

Aside from all of these considerations, you may want to take a close look at the actual materials that make up the home's present plumbing system, particularly if you are doing your total gut within the basic confines of the existing structure—not razing the house, but completely making it over inside. Older homes, say pre-1970s, probably have plumbing that is, depending on the age of the structure, predominantly piped with cast iron or galvanized pipe. The more modern materials are copper for the basic plumbing layout, particularly where regular access is likely to be neither convenient nor common; and PVC, where the owner will be able to have better access for maintenance and/or repair. PVC doesn't have the durability of copper, but it is generally less expensive, and is frequently used where design

Moneysaver

Having an in-home sprinkler system will usually gain homeowners a reduction in premiums on their fire insurance.

demands require larger pipes. Major drain and waste pipes are good examples of this.

The intended use of a particular part of the system will dictate what material is used. Copper is generally used for supply lines, while PVC or iron is used for drainage. Both avoid the typical problem that older pipes of the earlier materials suffer—gradual deposit buildup inside the pipes that ultimately leads to rusty water or reduced flow, and, eventually, a need to replace the pipe.

All of these extensive requirements for water and its many uses demand that the home's plumbing system be carefully thought out and expertly installed.

Structural

As with electrical and plumbing, modern design has resulted in a number of new concepts, materials, and processes for home construction. Better quality materials, some natural, some man-made, have found their way into the home construction indus-try over the last several years. Some are used due to their durability or safety effectiveness, while others have become com-mon due to their comparative ease of use or cost-effectiveness. Still others have made the homes in which they are used more able to withstand natural destructive events such as earthquakes or high winds.

When studs are nailed together or beams hung between walls, metal braces or hangers are nailed into each of the con-nected pieces of wood making up the stud framing or beams that are attached to the ceiling. This gives additional strength to the basic nailing or bolting that the affected beams or studs started with.

Construction of wooden homes in seismically active areas such as much of California and the area between St. Louis and Memphis is now commonly strengthened by the addition of shear walls when they are framed. Sheets of plywood are nailed across the stud framework, thus preventing extreme movement or twisting of the framing during an earthquake. By protecting against such movement, the likelihood of severe damage in a quake is lessened.

Another area that continues to rapidly change is that of structural materials. While wood is far from being eliminated in one form or another, more homes are being redone using steel studs for framing instead of wood. Also, the siding used, while most commonly remaining as some form of wood, has in the last several years seen the entry of such things as foam (similar to that used in white foam disposable coffee cups) or rammed earth. The latter technique uses actual clay-based earth that is structurally pre-formed for construction sections of the home's walls. Its benefits are its total resistance to insect infestation (beetle or termite) and fire, as well as its excellent insulating qualities. The cost is marginally higher than wood, but when the benefits are balanced against the costs to maintain wood against pests and the costs of installed insulation, there is little net difference.

Other commonly used items today are paint, shingles, and stain that are less susceptible to damage from the elements, thus lasting longer and, in some cases, conserving energy. Rain gutter systems and downspouts are now more commonly made of plastics or, in more expensive homes, copper, because these materials last longer than galvanized or nongalvanized metal.

Separately, as engineering techniques have evolved over the years, many homes are able to be safely built today that in years past were impossible or prohibitively expensive. These techniques find their way into such areas as foundations and cantilevered decks or upper stories. All can be considered in your project as the need dictates due to either the location of your project or your desires in terms of design.

Interior design details

This is the floor plan of the house as you do your flip. Depending on your intentions, budget, lot, and living area sizes, you will, with the assistance of your architect, determine the exact number, size, style, and shape of the rooms in the finished house. Therefore, I am not going to get into that very deeply at this point, other than to say that all of the commentary I've made up to this point about flips in general also applies here.

However, if you intend to add a second story, or expand by adding wings to the house, your expenses will climb accordingly. This is because you will have to either expand or strengthen/replace the foundation to accommodate your new structure. Also, you will have a great deal more material to purchase for the extra amount of floor area that will go into your enlarged home. You'll have made this decision when you decided what type of gut you were going to do, and determined a budget that would still leave you with a good profit.

Your choice of materials, cabinets, counters, and appliances for kitchens and baths (see Chapters 10 and 11) still applies here. The only additional concerns that you will have regarding these matters in a total gut over an intermediate flip is there is more work and cost involved in the project.

I briefly discussed skylights in Chapter 10 when I discussed cosmetic flips. What I said there applies equally to total guts—in some cases, even more so when the skylight design and its effects become a major focus of one part of the house.

Here's a good example: One of my clients did a total gut centered around a spiral staircase connecting the home's two floors. To increase the amount of light down the central shaft of the home, she installed a huge skylight directly above the staircase, letting light stream down the path of the staircase into the central rooms of the house.

External additions

When you are involved in a total gut in a higher-end locale, or can stand one or more "extras" that will return your investment and give you a bump in your profit, there are a number of items you may want to consider as a part of your finished project. A couple of these extras may also comfortably lend themselves to an intermediate flip. I'll lead off with those additions first and then proceed to others that will likely be worth considering only in a total gut.

The addition or reconstruction of a deck or patio, or multiples of either, always increases a home's desirability and attractiveness to prospective buyers. This is because these items add an extra lifestyle option to the prospective buyers' ownership of the home. By creating an indoor/outdoor flexibility to the utility of the home, its potential use becomes more varied and therefore more attractive to a larger number of possible buyers. If someone wants to barbeque, they can always set up the grill on the lawn, but a deck or flagstone patio gives the activity more permanence and specific definition while saving the lawn for other "greener" activities.

As with everything else in a flip, the type of material used, as well as style, determine the cost of this type of addition. But whatever the limits you place on this detail, it is an excellent extra to have to increase appeal to your potential market. Materials for decks or patios run the gamut from almost any type of wood through plastics and synthetics, to a broad variety of stone and tile.

In higher-end decks or patios, you may wish to have railings built in, as well as some type of bench seating. Both can be made to blend right in with the construction even if you are doing a very high-end patio with steel reinforced stonework as your predominant material.

Sidewalks and driveways are another area where investing a little extra money can increase your return. Falling into the area of curb appeal, improving the driveway and sidewalks provides

 Bright Idea

If you're building a deck or patio, consider having it plumbed for gas and water and wired for electrical outlets. Such planning gives a potential buyer the flexibility to use either a charcoal or gas grill, as well as water any plants on the deck or patio, and plug in lights for nighttime use of the area.

Watch Out!

For safety reasons, always replace broken or heavily cracked driveways and sidewalks.

a perfect opportunity for additional types of plantings to improve the overall appearance of the outside of the project.

Aside from the obvious, your choice of design and materials for this task is nearly endless. Starting with basic concrete or asphalt, you can quickly proceed to a huge choice of brick, stone, and cobblestone. All of these can be interspersed with wood accents and borders, or deliberately planted so a tiny line of grass or other greenery grows in the seams between the bricks or stones you use. You can also make the appearance more interesting by using a pattern when you lay the material. Examples are herringbone patterns for brick, or geometrics made from contrasting colored cobblestones. A local contractor I know has occasionally created a "stream" pattern in the middle of the driveway for its entire length by using contrasting colored stone to create the appearance of a flowing streambed down the center of the driveway.

While it's nice to have good relationships with one's neighbors, it's always a good thing to be able to have privacy when you want. A fenced-in back yard gives you this sense of privacy and adds to a home's value. Also, if you have a pool or hot tub, a fence is usually required for liability reasons, to protect you from a neighbor's young child innocently wandering in unnoticed one day and possibly drowning in your pool.

Recreational extras

Unless any of these already exist in a house on which you're doing an intermediate flip, let's look at some extras that you should consider only in a total gut, and then only when the price point of your market dictates it. These items include pools and hot tubs, tennis courts, and other athletic facilities. While these types of extras appeal to a broad range of people, only a certain market will pay for them.

As with everything else, consider your budget and your projected return when deciding whether to construct these extra features. Also take into account the location of the flip. For example, there are some geographical areas where only a small percentage of potential buyers have any interest in a pool, while in other sections of the country, every home seems to have a pool.

Similarly, while tennis courts, basketball courts, or putting greens may look good, keep in mind the price point of the potential buyer to avoid building something in as an extra that's only going to cost you money and cut into your profits. In a very high-end flip, extras such as a tennis court can be an excellent idea. But in a project directed at middle-income buyers, all such additions are likely to do is to kill your profits. If, given the local neighborhood and prevailing lifestyle, you still feel you have to have some sort of athletic facility as part of your finished project, consider a small sport court or basketball hoop area. Some of these can be done for under $10,000 when kept to a minimum of space and options.

Just the facts

- Make sure you obtain all necessary permits before you start work—it'll save you much time, expense, and aggravation later.

- Local codes can have a major effect on what you can and cannot do with your overall design. They should be carefully reviewed before you get underway.

- Simply by the nature of a total gut, your project will have much more extensive work on its systems—plumbing, heating, and electrical—than other types of flips.

- As you are doing a total gut, you have the opportunity to create a floor plan that conforms more closely to current lifestyles than the former home's layout may have done.

- Decks and patios by their nature always add desirability to a house, and thus, to its attraction to potential buyers. These items expand the home's utility to occupants.

- Special extras such as pools, tennis courts, or putting greens are excellent additions but probably only suitable for higher-end flips. Adding these to homes targeted at middle-income buyers will only cut into your profit.

PART IV

Doing the Work

GET THE SCOOP ON...
Assembling a team of professionals ▪ Working
with contractors ▪ Licensing, bonding, and other
considerations ▪ Entering into a partnership

Chapter 13

Picking Your Team

When anyone decides to put together a team or organization to handle a project, run a company, or work toward the completion of a common goal, he or she usually ends up with some organizational structure that could be laid out on a piece of paper. Depending on the type of activity and the group working on it, this organization usually has a name for the structure. In the corporate world, it is frequently referred to as a "plumbing chart," because when laid out on paper, it resembles the many pipes and connections in a plumbing layout of a building.

The military calls the setup a TO&E, or Table of Organization and Equipment. In the world of athletics, it's commonly called a team, pure and simple. I'll use the latter, but whatever you call it, it is the group of people with whom you will work to complete your flip.

Some parts of the team have already been mentioned in previous chapters, particularly Chapter 5, where I discussed costs and budgets. Depending on your intentions, you may break the team into two main groups, professionals and contractors, below the ownership level. While contractors are very often professionals at their specialty, I am reserving the term "professional" for the non-construction specialists on your team who, with the main exception of the Realtor and escrow or title officer, do most of their work before you begin construction.

The professionals

In the vast majority of cases, the professionals on your team will be made up of any or all of the following individuals:

- Attorney
- Accountant
- Banker
- Architect
- Realtor
- Escrow or title officer

Any of these may be single individuals or, as you and they feel necessary, more than one of a type. Each person performs a necessary function in your overall project designed either to protect you and your interests or to help you succeed in your project. Their professional designation would seem to make their responsibility obvious, but let's discuss each of them so that nothing is missed at this important phase of your project.

Keep in mind that there may be cases when you can do much of the work on your own, without having some of these people directly involved. For instance, in a cosmetic flip, you probably won't need the services of an architect. If you are handling all of your financial activities yourself other than getting the loan, you may choose to issue all checks and make all deposits. You may also decide, particularly if you have done a number of property transactions, that you can handle all of the drafting of contracts and related documentation for a purchase or sale without using an attorney. As you build your team, decide how large a team is necessary for you and your project, and then assemble it from there.

Attorney

While it is obvious that you have an attorney to handle all legal matters relating to your planned flip, exactly what does this amount to? The tasks vary from project to project, but, at a minimum, the attorney checks any contractual questions you may have with contractors and suppliers, as well as any issues that may arise with the local municipality regarding zoning and other ordinance matters affecting your flip.

Perhaps you become aware of an easement across the property you are planning to buy for the flip, or, once you own the property, a neighbor claims that the former owner promised him unfettered access to the forested area behind your property with access across the lot you now own. These are just a few of the issues you may need to have an attorney review and resolve. In some parts of the country where title is reviewed by an attorney, your attorney also carefully examines the chain of title to the property you have bought just to be certain that the person selling it to you legally owns it, and that there are no other potential clouds on that title that could affect your ownership at some later date.

If legal action is threatened or arises from any of these issues, your attorney will obviously be involved in working through the problem, hopefully before it becomes a full-blown lawsuit. Remember, by protecting your interests, the attorney is not only acting in court when it is necessary, but more often in any number of other out-of-court activities in order to avoid anything ever having to go to court.

Your attorney can also help you establish the legal vehicle under which you hold ownership of the property while you're

 Watch Out!

If an issue progresses to the point where you must go to court, the costs go up dramatically. Not only do the attorney's fees increase, but also the time you have the lender's money tied up and generating interest increases.

doing your work. If it's anything other than a sole ownership by you personally or a joint tenancy with your spouse or partner, it is likely that a legal structure for the ownership will be established by your attorney for you to use. It could be a partnership, a corporation, or a tenants-in-common format. Perhaps when you financed the purchase, you had the seller of the property take back a mortgage covering a portion of your purchase. Your attorney would have drawn up or reviewed the relevant documents, or had a hand in the process.

Accountant

The role the accountant plays depends entirely on how much direct control you maintain over the books, receipts, and expenditures for the project. If you process and sign all the checks written for any expenses related to the flip, the accountant has a less involved and less expensive responsibility. If the opposite is the case, then he or she is a more important team member.

It is most likely that you have your accountant maintaining the books for the flip, not only to allow you ongoing oversight of how the project is going as related to your budget and finances, but also to keep your daily expenses under control. The accountant's work is also focused toward having accurate records available for the preparation of your tax returns. Whether flipping is your regular business or a side source of income will determine what kind of tax return you file. Your accountant can advise you.

Even if the accountant is only maintaining records for income and expense from the project, there are individual accounts under these general classifications that he or she keeps up. If you're doing anything other than a total gut, and the project time frame carries from one tax year into the next, you may be able to claim depreciation on your property. If that is so, your accountant knows it and can calculate it for you to use on your tax returns.

If the accountant is responsible for drawing all checks to your suppliers and contractors, he or she also has to review any claims for payment before drawing the appropriate checks, just to ensure that proper payments are being made and to the appropriate individuals. In this scenario, it is also likely that your accountant is reviewing and balancing your account statements from the bank as they relate to the flip. Depending on the depth of your accountant's involvement in the process, you may even have him or her reviewing the escrow documents in your behalf where these documents cover money paid into or out of the escrow.

Another task that your accountant handles is the preparation of financial statements that your lender requires prior to your loan application, and, in some cases, as you progress through the development and completion of the flip. The former statements are obvious in purpose. They tell the lender if you can afford the loan. The other "in process" statements may be a requirement of the loan as a way of keeping the lender comfortable with your progress as you go forward on the work on the flip.

Banker

The role of the banker is usually limited to one or two tasks: handling your operating account for the venture, and, if the same particular bank is the lender on the project, overseeing the loan or loans related to the development. I won't discuss either role in too much detail because both are, for the most part, pretty obvious. If this banker holds the paper on your venture, he or she oversees all of the documentation required by the bank to protect its interests, such as a mortgage, related loan documents, and promissory note.

Beyond the banker's responsibility for the institution's proper handling of your account, he or she may also handle other duties for you from time to time. These could involve wire transfers for certain payments you need to make faster than the normal mailing of a check allows, or letters of credit to secure a purchase or payment for some part of the development.

These are additional services that a bank can and does normally offer in the course of business for its clients. They basically put the bank's name and resources in the position of the client for the particular transaction being handled, with reimbursement to the bank coming from the client's account after the transaction has been completed. All such extra transactions have their own fee schedule, but in all cases, they are very reasonable for the service provided.

Architect

The architect draws your plans for the construction portion of your venture. Obviously, if you are doing a purely cosmetic flip, you probably won't require the services of an architect. However, any project beyond this easiest of flips, where construction is required, definitely requires an architect's input. The more involved your project gets from that point on, the more involved the architect is in your development. While he or she obviously produces your blueprints, in the case of a total gut, where everything is torn down to bare ground or just to the foundation, and you may possibly be expanding that area as well, the architect does much more, including preparing site plans, drainage plans, and "working drawings" of the appropriate areas of the planned structure. For a total gut, he or she may also do a series of renderings of the finished structure. These drawings are used both as a part of your permit application and for any marketing literature for the project, both paper and electronic.

Another service many architects provide for their clients is recommending materials and providing samples of the various materials contemplated for the project. Such samples are often used as part of the permit application process, both in dealing with the permitting authorities, and also at any public hearings on permits. If the local authorities require that you make changes in your design before they grant you your permits, the architect also draws the revised blueprints and accompanying drawings. These revised plans are then added to your application for the permits.

Bright Idea

Ask your architect if he or she can provide reduced sets of the plans and renderings to go with your Realtor's marketing materials when the time comes to sell the finished structure.

Realtor

The final two professionals on your team have already put in time and effort on your behalf. They did so on your acquisition of the building that you are planning to flip. The Realtor reappears later in the process to assemble a marketing program for the property, based on discussions with you and possibly your architect about the changes you have made in the building since he or she helped you acquire it.

The Realtor helps you prepare any disclosures, legally mandated or otherwise, that you must provide to potential buyers when the home is placed on the market. He or she also makes recommendations for preparing the home to show as well as possible to potential buyers and their agents at market time. This activity includes reviewing your home's curb appeal, staging, and presentation to the market. (I'll discuss this in more detail in Chapters 16 and 17.) Additionally, based on his knowledge of the market at the time, the Realtor helps you decide on the proper price to put on your finished property.

Escrow or title officer

The escrow or title officer oversees any activity related to the escrow established for the sale of your property. Depending on where in the country you are located, this can be as little as handling the transfer of the buyer's funds to you for purchase of the house and making sure the deed is recorded for the new owner, to as much as handling funds, preparing title reports, overseeing closing documents, and a raft of other tasks (see Chapter 17).

Contractors

The contractors are the folks who actually do the work on the project. There are many ways to handle this part of the venture. You can act as your own general contractor and pick your individual subcontractors as each phase of the project develops, or you can hire a general contractor and leave everything up to him or her as to which and how many subcontractors are involved. The general contractor may take direct responsibility for a certain specific number of the systems or components of the project and sub out only the electrical, for instance. On the other hand, he or she may engage subcontractors for every part of the project. In theory, every separate component or system in the house could have its own subcontractor—you could have separate subcontractors for plumbing, electrical, roofing, foundation, paving, painting, and so on right through the entire project. This decision is one that either you or your general contractor will make.

The role of the general contractor

Whether you retain one or do it yourself, the job of the general contractor is to engage the subcontractors to be used on the different phases of the project and oversee their work, ensuring that everything is done according to code and plans. In many cases, the general contractor does some of the actual physical work. Clearly, if you act as your own general contractor, you won't be doing this, unless you personally have a great deal of expertise and experience in the field.

Whether you act as your own general contractor or hire one, a crucial part of that role is to expedite the job. This involves

 Moneysaver

If you have the knowledge and experience, and feel comfortable doing so, consider acting as your own general contractor. It's one less person to whom you'll have to pay a profit margin.

coordinating the timing of getting materials and subcontractors on the job. For example, the plumber and electrician need to be done with their work before the sheet rocker is scheduled to come in. If they are not, the sheet rocker will start a different job, be off on his timing to your job, and then you will likely have to reschedule the painter. This goes on over the life of the entire job.

Licensed and bonded

If you choose to hire a professional general contractor for your development, there are two things you should be absolutely certain of. First, he or she must be licensed as a contractor in your state. All states have a licensing system for contractors, and some take it a bit beyond the simple status of licensing. In California, for example, it is a misdemeanor for anyone not licensed as a contractor to perform any construction or construction-related work on a property that costs $500 or more. Violators risk fines and jail time. Before you hire your contractor(s), ask to see his or her license and note the details for your own protection.

Now, clearly, there are unlicensed individuals just as capable of doing quality construction work as a licensed contractor. For whatever reason, they have decided not to go through the process of obtaining a license. They usually cost less than a licensed contractor, and the good ones are almost always fully booked as far as work goes. However, that does not lessen potential liability that may accrue, depending on the law in your area, both to you and your unlicensed people.

A contractor, as well as any subcontractors on the job, should also be bonded. Without a license, no contractor, no matter how good his work, will be able to obtain a bond. It's all well and good to go with individuals who aren't bonded, but if something goes wrong with their work due to poor workmanship, the absence of a bond leaves you holding the bag. If something goes wrong with an unbonded contractor's work after the sale, your hope of receiving nothing but praise for your project from the buyer may disappear, along with a good part of what you

Watch Out!

Before you hire them, be certain all contractors are licensed, bonded, and carry workman's comp insurance. Subcontractors should also be bonded. Ask to see proof of both the bond and the individual's license, and make sure they're current.

thought was your profit. Just as in the case of the license, ask to see proof of your contractor's bond, and, as with the license, note the details: bonding company, contact info, and, if indicated, the amount of the bond. Depending on the laws in your state, you should also be sure that your contractor(s) have workman's compensation insurance. It protects you against claims by a worker if they are injured on the job and cannot work. The workman's comp pays them a certain amount.

Why hire a general contractor?

There are benefits to hiring a good general contractor rather than trying to do it yourself. General contractors may be aware of below-market-cost material from their suppliers that becomes available on a one-time-only basis. Maybe they can get a certain quality of siding at 20 percent below cost because their supplier ordered too much as a result of miscalculating his customers' needs. Perhaps the cabinet maker working on your kitchen and baths knows of a perfect set of bird's-eye maple cabinets of the type you desire at a large discount because the job they were ordered for was cancelled. Usually savings of this kind get passed on, at least partially, to you by the contractor. While you should not make the hiring decision on a general contractor based on such possibilities—and that's all they are—it's something you may want to consider when you make your decision.

Subcontractors

If you hire a general contractor and leave the subcontracting choices to him or her, the general contractor will check to ensure that the subs have their proper licenses, bonds, and, where appropriate, workman's comp. You should still ask to see proof of these things, however. This is just a further protection for you against potential liability should something go wrong during the process of the job.

This brings us to another area where caution is required. When your general contractor has engaged various subcontractors, you usually pay the total owed to the general contractor, who in turn pays the various subs what they are owed. Just as you get a receipt from your general contractor when you pay him or her, you should also insist on receipts from each sub who is paid. This is to protect you down the road from any mechanics liens placed on your project to secure an unpaid job by any of those subs. Alternately, you can pay the general contractor what he or she is owed, and then pay the subs directly. Whichever way you choose to go, make sure you get a receipt for the payments.

In some cases a subcontractor may hire his or her own sub—a sub-sub, if you will. Perhaps there is some small part of a sub's job that is very detailed and, although the sub is capable of doing it, there is someone who specializes solely on that one type of work. If there is enough room in the contract for his overall responsibility, the sub may go ahead and engage the sub-sub.

As with the other levels of contractor, ensure that a sub-sub has a license, is bonded, and, where that sub-sub has others beside him, has workman's comp insurance. One additional item applies in this case. Retain for yourself the approval for any sub-subs the subs may wish to engage. As in the case of subs, make sure you receive proof that they have, in fact, been paid by their hiring sub, or better yet, insist that you be the one to pay them.

Paying the contractors

You can pay your contractors one of two ways. You can pay on a bid for the job, or you can pay for time and materials. Each method is just what it sounds like. Usually, you'll go by the bid method. However, there are times when the time and materials method is preferable. For example, when some very detailed or technical work on a part of the project is needed, it may be cheaper in the long run to have the contractor work on time and materials than under a bid. This is because if the individual is very good at his or her craft, he or she may be able to finish it correctly in less time than someone else, and thus cost less on an hourly basis. Similarly, the contractor may be able to obtain materials below prevailing market prices through connections in his or her area of the market. It won't always work out, but it certainly is worth discussing when you're interviewing a contractor.

Working with a partner

You may be the sole owner of the project, taking on all the financial risk and receiving all of the hoped-for rewards, or you may wish to have one or more partners to spread the risk a bit. This is a decision that you should make after carefully considering your financial situation and your appetite for risk.

If you decide to partner with one or more of your contractors, there are certain benefits:

- You have an expert in the contractor's specialty working with you who has a direct stake in the ultimate outcome of the venture beyond his or her profit. This is usually good incentive for top-quality work on the project.

- As with any partner, it spreads the risks.

- The contractor is likely to focus more attention on your project above any others because of his or her personal interest in the outcome.

 Watch Out!

If you decide to do your venture with partners, don't do it on a handshake. Have an attorney draft a partnership agreement that spells out each partner's specific obligations, liabilities, and benefits from the inception of the arrangement. Even the best friendships will quickly unravel when things go wrong and there is nothing more than a verbal agreement binding the partners.

Cautions that you should keep in mind are the same as in any partnership. Be certain of limits to your liability through the partnership. Don't allow your participation as partners broaden into responsibility for any other projects of your contractor-partner. Also, make certain that your funds, be they capital or borrowed money, don't get diverted to some other project or need of your contractor-partner. This last problem does crop up from time to time, and the best way to avoid it is to be very familiar with your potential partner before you decide to make him or her your partner. The basic rule is that if you wouldn't feel comfortable being in business with the individual, then don't enter into a partnership with that person in your flip. Keep the person as a hired contractor. That assumes that you believe the person to be a quality contractor whom you can trust for that responsibility.

Just the facts

- Carefully assemble your team, remembering to build it in conjunction with the degree of complexity and size of your project.

- Don't include people whose work merely duplicates the work you'd normally do.

- Decide at the start whether you want a general contractor or if you would rather be your own general contractor and hire the subs yourself.

- Make certain all contractors working on the project are currently licensed and bonded and have workers' comp (if applicable) get receipts from everyone whenever they are paid.

- If you do a project with a partner, have a carefully drafted partnership agreement drawn up by your attorney.

GET THE SCOOP ON...
What to do first, for any kind of flip ▪ Scheduling
considerations for cosmetic, intermediate,
and total-gut flips ▪ Dealing with unexpected
problems ▪ Progress inspections

Doing the Construction

Well, now you're underway. You've done all of the preparation work, the "soft" background things for your venture, and it's time to begin the actual physical work. The obvious question is, "So, where do I begin?" It's a logical question, and one that will be easy to answer no matter which type of flip you are undertaking. Regardless of whether you're on your first flip and, consequently, doing a cosmetic one, or, at the other extreme, involved in your latest in a long line of flips and doing a total gut, your first steps will be the same.

Establish a work schedule

The first thing you will do, ideally in consultation with at least some of your contractors, if not all of them, is to establish a work schedule. There are several reasons why having a schedule is important:

- It establishes a specific orderly progression through the work right up to and including its completion.

- It minimizes materials lying unused on the site long before you are ready for them.

- It keeps the interest from accruing too rapidly on your
  loan due to down time from materials not available for use
  when you need them or subcontractors being unavailable
  when you are ready for their part of the project.

When you have a specific schedule, everyone involved in the
venture knows more or less exactly when each part of the job is
scheduled, how much time has been allotted for it, and where
each task fits into the overall project. I am not implying that
there are never changes or exceptions made once a schedule is
finalized. Unforeseen events can sometimes cause delays that
impact your planned schedule.

Perhaps upon opening an interior wall in the master suite,
you discover an infestation of boring beetles that has done
major damage to the studs in that wall, necessitating replacement of all of those studs and related framing. Due to the location, it was never discovered when you did your inspections
when you acquired the property. But it is there and now must be
dealt with.

On the positive side, perhaps your general contractor was
able to acquire some first-quality siding already prepped at a
price equal to unprepped siding. The only catch is that he had
to commit to taking it two months before you will need it. In this
case, having it lying on the site early will likely be worthwhile
because it will save some money in the long run.

The point is, you should have a definite schedule for the
work, and, as much as reasonably possible, keep to it. But if
there are good reasons to step outside the schedule at some
point, then it may very well be okay to do so.

Empty the house

The second step is also applicable on all types of flips. It may
seem obvious, but experience shows that it is still worth stating:
The house must be empty when you begin work. "Empty"
means no one must be living there once work begins. It also
means that all belongings normally found inside a house

Watch Out!

Once the house has been emptied, you can place some of your tools and equipment in the home for convenience. If you're doing a total gut, though, you'll probably want to wait until you've completed any demolition before leaving valuable tools and equipment inside the structure.

should have been removed. Clear out all furniture, clothing, art, dishes, decorations—everything that the former resident may have had inside the house and/or garage—get rid of it!

In the case of an intermediate flip or total gut, this rule also applies to the outside. Remove all yard ornaments and lawn decorations. (You might have to make exceptions where a huge gazebo, spa and deck, or heavy stone fountain makes removal impractical. In this case, cover them or protect them in some way so as not to risk damage, flying paint, or some other form of harm to the object.)

Order materials and schedule subcontractor work

The next step is to order all materials, and schedule the work for all of the various subcontractors. If you're using the services of a general contractor, this is something that he or she will work on for you or with you. As part of the ordering, the arrival of all of the different materials can be set to coincide as much as possible with the part of the schedule when the work that they relate to is scheduled to be undertaken. If some materials require a lead time of over two weeks, you may want to schedule their arrival two to four weeks early to avoid delays from things not arriving at their originally expected time. This won't always be possible, but it should be prearranged as much as possible.

Some materials may be backordered and unavailable for use when you'd prefer. In that case, other parts of the project work can be completed, as long as doing so won't cause any problems in completing the section you're forced to work around. The main point is that you want framing lumber available when it's time to do the framing. You want windows when you're ready to hang them, roofing materials when it's time for the roof, cabinets when it's their turn, and so on.

Keep in mind that the more involved your flip is, the more materials and workers you'll have to schedule. This means more to keep on schedule. Any major delays in one or two areas can have a much wider effect on the overall project because there are so many additional parts that may become involved as a result. Delays in materials arriving on schedule and the availability of the subcontractors to work on that phase of the project can cost additional money in terms of interest from any construction loan sums already advanced for the venture, as well as the possibility of completing the project after the market conditions have changed, thereby making it more difficult for you to receive as much for your flip as you'd first projected.

> ❝Here's my rule of thumb: Materials will arrive later than promised. Work will take longer than anticipated. Contractors will not be able to start work when you are ready for them.❞
>
> —Robert, experienced flipper

It's at this point that the schedule begins to differ with the type of flip you undertake. As you will see in the following sections of this chapter, the different nature of each type of flip will mandate different procedures.

Cosmetic flip schedule

At this point, the first thing you will do is prep work on the house to get it ready for its cosmetic improvements. There will be little, if any, structural work to undertake for preparation. Any work on the shell of the structure that you may do will be relatively minor. For example, if you're going to add a small skylight over the kitchen or in the master suite, your work on the shell of the building will be limited to cutting the hole in the roof to install the skylight.

Beyond this, most of your prep work will be the type that is typical for any painting or wallpapering that you would do in any house. Similarly, your prep work for replacing the flooring—be it wood, tile, carpet, or a combination of any of these—will be the same as what would be performed in any home where that work was being done by a homeowner.

In the case of painting or putting new wallpaper on the interior walls, the walls will first be cleaned, and, if applicable, stripped of old wallpaper. Any cracks or holes will be filled and sanded smooth. If walls are to be painted, a primer coat of paint will be applied once the walls are cleaned of old paper.

On the outside of the house, before any painting is begun, the house will probably be power-washed and scraped to remove layers of dirt, old peeling paint, and spider webs or other unwanted debris that has attached itself to the surfaces. Once this has been completed, cracks and small holes in the surface will be filled and sealed. Caulking of any small gaps, where necessary, will also be completed at this time.

At the same time, any windows being replaced will be installed or repaired, so that when you finally get to the part of the schedule for painting, they will be ready for their coat of paint.

Another item of pre-painting preparation that will be handled here is the protection of plants and shrubbery. Unless all existing plantings are projected for removal and replacement—in which case you needn't worry about them—you and your team should carefully cover or otherwise protect the existing plantings from such things as dripping paint or primer, breakage from tools or ladder placement, or damage from any falling debris as the siding is prepped for painting. This is very important, because these plants are an important part of the home's curb appeal. Having to replace damaged or dead plants will cut into your profits. Ignoring them will likely reduce what a buyer is willing to pay for the home. If there are some plants that you definitely do not want, or think just won't work with your project, take them out. Otherwise, protect existing plants.

Whatever else is planned for your cosmetic flip, you schedule the paint for the first step so you won't risk damaging new wallpaper or having to spend time (and money) cleaning new tile that you just installed. Then, once the painting has been completed, you can proceed with the other parts of your cosmetic restoration of the property. While wallpaper paste, tile mastic, or grout can be splattered on painted woodwork, it is relatively easier to clean up than the other way around. This is partly because paint, due to its consistency, is more likely to cover a wider swath by spattering or spilling than wallpaper paste, tile mastic, or grout.

If you are doing new cabinetry, even something as simple and inexpensive as refacing, you certainly don't want to install the new wood and then have someone spill a bucket of paint over one entire side of your newly updated kitchen. While it can be cleaned off, there is always the danger that the cleaning process will damage the finish of the new cabinet or leave a small area of paint that couldn't be cleaned up, thus harming the appearance of the wood.

Similarly, if you drip or spatter paint on the new drawer pulls or cabinet handles, it can be a real pain to have to remove the affected fixture and manually clean the spattered paint from its surface. This is particularly true if the handle or pull is not a smooth surface, but curved or twisted. Chances are you will not be able to get all of the paint off the sprayed drawer pull. The other option is equally unappealing. You can't manually remove the spattered paint, so you leave the affected pieces soaking in a paint remover solution for an hour or so. When you take the fixtures out to dry and reinstall them, you note that while the paint is gone, so is the finish that the fixture originally had. You then have to go out and purchase a new one to replace this one.

Bright Idea

If your cosmetic flip includes new plantings, flower beds, or new sod, do that work last, when all of the work on the structure is complete. This will prevent possible damage from workers trampling in or on these features.

Admittedly, one or two fixtures shouldn't make or break your budget. But it's a colossal waste of your valuable time to have to do this.

Likewise, it's a waste of time and money to have to remove spattered or spilled paint from new outside lighting fixtures or from the house numbers you installed. Wait until you've finished all painting before mounting the lights in place and screwing the address numbers on the front of the house.

Intermediate flip schedule

In this type of flip, some of the elements of a schedule will also have a commonality with the total gut. If you recall, what separates the intermediate flip from a total gut is primarily the degree of work on the house. Much of the same work is done on both, but whereas the entire house is undertaken as part of a total gut, in the case of an intermediate flip, this type of major work is largely limited to one or two major portions of the structure. I'll discuss the elements of the intermediate flip schedule here, and note where they are common to the total gut schedule when we get to the total gut schedule portion of this chapter.

As with the cosmetic flip schedule, all materials will be ordered with planned delivery times laid out to coincide with the time of work when you expect to need them for the construction or installation. However, as I've already noted, if you're looking at something that has a longer order time, it's wise to add two to four weeks to its order time to cover yourself against unexpected delivery delays.

Demolition

Here you begin the first real substantial physical work—demolition. Any and all demo work you plan to do should be done before even the smallest part of reconstruction begins. It's messy, dirty, and, if not properly managed, can harm new materials to be installed. So get this out of the way first. The amount of time and tools you may need will obviously depend on the overall scope of your project and, to a degree, the type of existing structure you are working with. Of course, there will be less demo work on a single-story building than on a multi-story one, even in the case of an intermediate flip.

If you're doing a smaller intermediate flip, with only the kitchen and bath(s) being redone, you may even get most, if not all, of the demo work out of the way in one or two days. One client of mine handled this on her latest project by having a weekend demo party/barbeque at the site, with the bulk of the work accomplished by about a half dozen people on the first day of the weekend. You'd be amazed how much benefit you can get out of a couple of six packs each of beer and soda, and a few dozen sausages or burgers and buns.

However, if you choose to serve alcohol at such a party, a few cautions are in order. Use common sense on the amount of beer consumed by the workers, and make sure that your liability insurance on the property covers guests in any "normal" activity on the property. You'd hate to have your expected profits eaten up in a lawsuit from one of your friends after he gets injured by a falling section of sheetrock or broken glass from the window he was removing. Let's face it, even in the most carefully run situations,

 Watch Out!

Demo parties can be fun and save money, but be VERY careful about potential liability from those at the party having too much to drink and then injuring themselves or someone else there or on the way home. Your savings could evaporate in a large lawsuit.

injuries can occur. On this particular one, I opened up a nice deep gash between my thumb and forefinger with the wrong end of a crowbar while removing some kitchen cabinets.

More substantial demo work—whether because it's a larger house, or you're doing more of the structure as part of the venture—can take a few more days, possibly the better part of a week. In any event, get it done, and have all of the debris hauled away from the site before beginning the construction work.

Basic structural work

Next on the timeline is the foundation. It is unlikely you'll be doing much, if any, foundation work on the typical intermediate flip, unless you're adding a room as part of the project. For example, if you have decided to redo the kitchen and baths on your project house and add a new wing with an office or den and half-bath, you'll have to do the foundation for that new wing.

Similarly, in the typical intermediate flip, your framing work is likely to be relatively small as a portion of the overall work you'll be undertaking. Most framing work in an intermediate flip will be limited to either changing the layout of the floor plan of the existing house or adding on a room or wing to that existing structure.

In the former case, the redesign of the floor plan will have you framing up internal walls to define the redesigned floor plan, or to do the framing of external walls where you're enlarging one or more rooms in the house. You may be taking one very large room and cutting it into another bedroom and separate office or convertible den.

Perhaps you're going to expand the master suite into a larger one, adding a huge walk-in closet and spa area. As the existing structure has no room for this, you're planning to knock out the existing rear wall and expand the area of the room in that direction. Maybe your planned flip has you pretty much maintaining the existing floor plan, but adding on a separate wing off the existing living room/dining room area to allow a new den and media room with its own bathroom. In addition to the framing for the wing, you'll probably find yourself framing in a small hallway to lead into the new wing.

Once you do the framing, whatever the layout may be, the next thing on your schedule will be covering the external walls that the framing supports. On the exterior walls, you'll first be attaching plywood or particle board sheeting to provide a smooth surface for the external covering surface, either siding, stucco, or shingles. Once that has been accomplished, you'll attach that external cover surface.

This is also when most of the windows will be installed. If the specific windows you want for your venture will not be available at this point of the construction, you can use sheets of plywood nailed across the window openings as a temporary remedy. Covering the interior of the walls will come a bit later on in the work, as I'll discuss later in this chapter.

Now that the structure is once again fully laterally enclosed from the elements, animals, and any unwanted passersby, you will come to the next scheduled item on your plan. That is to finish the enclosing by adding on and/or replacing any roofing that your plans require. Obviously, if you've enlarged the floor area or added a wing, you'll be adding to the existing roof. Depending on the age of the existing roof and the materials, you may either match the existing roof or replace it altogether. This is an item that should have figured into your plans when you first began your planning on this house.

Another thing to take into consideration on the roof: If you are enlarging the floor area, thus requiring some new roofing work to be undertaken, you may find out that even though the

 Watch Out!

Beware of removing any walls that are load-bearing walls. These areas must be re-engineered to provide new support for the load that's no longer supported by the removed wall. Check with an expert.

existing roof you had planned to keep is in good condition and still has 10 or 15 years' life left, you'll have to replace the entire roof anyway, as opposed to just adding new roofing over the expanded area of the house. This is most common when the color of the existing roofing cannot be matched with the same quality material to the newly added roofing. It's an extra expense, but you must add it. Nothing will turn off a potential buyer faster than seeing two different color roofs on the same house. It immediately tells her that part of the house is "old" and part is "new."

While you are at this stage, with walls and attic opened up, you should add insulation. Many local codes require it, and, even if it's not required, it is a great source of energy conservation for the finished structure.

Again, this is something that should have been looked into during the planning stages, although it is admittedly one area that frequently gets overlooked when planning a flip. The thinking may be, "I'm adding a new wing, so I'll need to expand the roof. This roof has more than 15 years left on it, so I'll just have the same type of roof used for the new area." Rarely does anyone think to ask if that color is still marketed in the same material. However, if you're going to be doing some roofing, it should be one of the first questions you ask your roofing contractor.

Operating systems

The next item on your schedule should be the operating systems of the house: plumbing, electrical, and heating/air conditioning. Although I say "next," you can have these systems going in while you are enclosing the house with outer walls and roof. If you have the manpower, it'll save on overall time expended.

Plumbing

Where necessary to support increased uses such as more modernized, better-equipped kitchen or baths, as well as the possible addition of a half-bath or a wet bar in a den or office, the plumbing system will have to be expanded to support these new uses, and possibly heavily upgraded. You may find yourself going from old cast iron or galvanized pipes to copper in many places. New piping is largely copper, with some areas seeing PVC. A new bath will require not only new piping, but also a new connection to the waste disposal line of the house. The various new plumbing fixtures planned for these additions will come later in the construction, once the walls, counters, and floors are in place.

In some areas, the addition of internal fire prevention sprinklers may be necessary. This will be something you will have been told when you sought your permits. Usually, a specialized plumbing contractor handles this item.

Electrical

Similarly, any new, redesigned, or expanded rooms will require new electrical outlets. Perhaps all the outlets in the existing home are two-pronged. Today's standard is three-pronged grounded outlets. Additionally, most, if not all, areas of the United States have safety codes requiring any outlets near a water source or use area such as a sink or bathtub to be equipped with a device that cuts off power to the outlet if there is a short circuit in the line at that point. This is called a GFCI, or ground fault circuit interrupter, and its purpose is to prevent electric shock to anyone using that outlet. Additionally, codes require a minimum number of outlets on each wall, as well as dedicated circuits for most major kitchen appliances.

Beyond the new outlets required by the redesign of the house, it is likely in any reasonably sized intermediate flip you will have to add a sub-panel, at a minimum, or, in some cases, even increase the size of the main electrical panel by replacing the existing one with a larger one to handle the expected increased demands on the electrical system that the remodeled structure will require. The size of the panel is important because it is the equipment that receives the electrical current from the utility company's source outside the house and then directs it to all of the various locations inside the structure where it is needed at any given time.

Bright Idea

In our increasingly high-tech world, new demands for electricity seemingly pop up daily. Many higher-end flips are including special wiring for computer systems, telecommunications, and state-of-the-art entertainment systems that go far beyond "standard" electrical capabilities of our homes of just a few years ago.

Another aspect of the home's electrical system is added wiring for additional lighting sources that the redesign may require. These can be ceiling, wall, or any combination thereof. In some redesigned kitchens or baths, there will even be special internal cabinet lighting setups

Heating and air conditioning

No house would be complete without adequate heating. In warmer regions, you can add the absolute necessity of air conditioning. While in most intermediate flips, you may not be adding or changing the heating and/or air conditioning that already exists, you very well may be adding increased ducting for that system. If you are either expanding or redesigning a room, or adding a new wing or room, you will want that room to have the same quality and availability of heating and cooling as the rest of the house. The only reasonable way to do this is by adding the appropriate amount of new ducting to carry the heat or cool air to those areas.

If, because of limitations created by the location or design of an added room or wing, it is prohibitively expensive to add new ducting to the system, or it would make the existing system less efficient overall, you may find it more effective and less costly to invest in a heating or cooling system just to serve that area of the finished house. My own house has exactly that situation.

Interior walls

By this point, you may have figured out the reason you didn't put up the new sheetrock as soon as the framing and siding were completed. Had you done so, you would have made it very difficult, if not impossible, to do the installation work on the various systems of the house. You would not have been able to run and secure the necessary wires, pipes, and ducts the various operating systems required, and the cutting of the locations for the usable outlets, be they electrical or water, might have been in the wrong places.

Once the systems are all installed, however, all of this becomes very easy. You will know exactly where each electrical socket and switch will be located, and thus, where to cut an opening in the sheetrock for the outlet that you've already installed. Similarly, you will be able to determine with little difficulty where to cut through the sheetrock as you install it in the kitchen and bathrooms where the appropriate plumbing fixtures have been attached according to the intended use of that location. Heating/air conditioning vent outlet locations will also be easy to locate and cut.

Flooring and finishing

At this point, you've done most of the structural updating. All that's left with the building itself is to do any flooring work that you've planned, add trim such as moldings, and paint or tile as your plans dictate. The first thing that you'll do is likely to be the flooring. Whether it's new hardwood, stone, or tile, this is the time that you'll install it.

Simultaneously with the floor installation, you can have the tile installed in bath/shower enclosures, as well as on counters in the baths and kitchen. Any new cabinetry can be installed, as I outlined in the earlier section on cosmetic flip schedules. Once installed, the counters, where applicable, will sit neatly on top of them. As far as the bathrooms are concerned, this is also

 Watch Out!

If you're planning to install wall-to-wall carpet, save it for after the painting to avoid getting any paint drips and stains on the carpet.

Moneysaver

It is always a good idea to have your painter try the color on a small area of one of the walls before painting an entire room. This is a lot cheaper than having him or her repaint the room if you find you don't like the color.

when you'll be installing any glass shower enclosures as well as new plumbing fixtures.

Now that you have completed the bulk of the construction work on the house, you can do the painting. Inside or outside; do it in whatever order you prefer, or, if your painter has the manpower, or you're using different contractors for each task, do the interior and exterior painting simultaneously. A good painter is very valuable not only for his or her capability in doing the painting, but also for his or her expertise in preparation of the job. Anyone who's had a few painting jobs completed, as well as anyone who's completed them, will tell you that in every case, preparation is at least as important, if not more so, than the actual painting.

Once it's time to paint, the painter will spend time working with you and, if you have one, your color consultant, to get just the right shade of paint in each location he or she is to paint. If you are one of those folks who really has very little appreciation of what colors are best in a given situation, or for a particular design, it is money well spent to engage the services of a color consultant to help guide you in the selection of a color scheme for both the exterior and interior of the completed structure. They can be a bit expensive on an hourly basis, but usually one or two hours should solve all of your problems with color.

Once the interior painting has been completed, you can have the floor and crown moldings installed. Ideally, these will have been painted outside individually before installation, then brought in to the proper room and installed. At this stage in the process, you can have the wall-to-wall carpet installed wherever you have planned to have it installed.

Once all of this has been finished, you can add the final interior touches. This is when you'll install all of your new cabinet and drawer fixtures, as well as any lighting fixtures. It's also the time when you'll do any property-specific final touches.

For example, if you're planning to change the appearance of the fireplace in the living room because you think that red brick is too rustic looking for the high-tech design you've created in that part of the house, this is when you'll reface the fireplace. In the same vein, if the simple and small mantelpiece over the fireplace in the family room looks too cheap, this is when you can install the new mantel and fireplace surround that you found at the local fireplace design and supply store. To give a more elegant appearance to a living room, one of my clients added a beautiful hand-carved antique surround to a fireplace in a living room that made a dramatic difference in the room's overall appearance. The surround had previously been in a century-old Victorian home that had been demolished.

Outside the house

Well, you've finished the house. Now, let's make sure the yard lives up to the image and impression you want to create. Structurally, you could add a deck or two, or possibly a patio. You could even install a hot tub. However, remember that you are adding expense in an area that usually gains some extra income, but on a less than one-to-one ratio. My advice is to keep those extras to a minimum. If you do a small deck or patio off the living room, don't go overboard. Perhaps you'll match the width of the living room it borders, but not have it go more than 8 or 10 feet laterally from the outer wall of the room. Then spend time on your gardens.

 Bright Idea

If you're spending good money on new plantings as part of the landscaping, consider installing some form of irrigation system.

If the existing gardens are well maintained and have a good selection of plants and flowers, you may not wish to do much here. On the other hand, if you either tore out much of what passed as a garden during your demo stage, or think that what's there is pretty minimal, you should opt for a good combination of green shrubs and bushes and flowering plants. Ideally, you want the flowering ones to be in bloom at the time your finished creation goes on the market. If that's not possible, be certain that whatever you plant is as lush and green as possible so that the garden looks appealing. If there is a large tree on the property fairly close to the house, you may want to ring it with floral plants.

Whether you decide to plant a hedge depends on your opinion as well as what the norm is in the area where you do your project. While I have seen some hedges that I liked in the front of a house, my general preference is to not have one in front. I'd rather have one along a common boundary with the neighboring yard or in the rear of the house.

My preference in front of a house is a nice lush green lawn. If the lawn that was there fits the description, then keep it. If not, have new sod professionally installed. You don't need a landscape architect to oversee the basics of an appealing yard and lawn.

One landscaping expert I know, Megan, notes that when it comes to mature trees on the property, you shouldn't remove healthy ones. Rather, she suggests that they be manicured or thinned as necessary to get that "sculptured" look. By the way, when she uses the word "sculptured" in this case, she is not talking about topiary; she is referring to the best appearance of a well-tended mature tree as an accent to the beauty of a property.

> ❝A beautiful yard attracts [interest]. I like to use colorful flowers to get that beauty. The colors don't necessarily have to match the home's color. You don't have to spend a lot of money to achieve a nice effect.❞
>
> —Megan, stager and color expert

When it comes to yard ornaments, different people have different opinions. If the purpose is to accent the appearance of the house without overwhelming it, then some ornamentation is perfectly fine. Too much takes away from the house and can actually be a negative. Items of sculpture or wind chimes are best left to the taste of the ultimate buyer. You may, in certain cases, have a garden sculpture or two, but generally the rule is don't.

Make sure to keep any outside accent material in the same architectural style as the house that it sits in front of. Few combinations look as bad as Mexican pavers in front of a traditional English cottage or Victorian house or a brick walkway leading up to a Mediterranean house. These styles conflict. If you intend to do something more than basic paving material, use something for your walks and/or drive that complements the architectural design.

Total gut schedule

Many of the subjects I just discussed in the previous sections will also apply in a total gut. In most cases, the only difference between the two is that there's more of the work involved in more places in the house in the total gut than the intermediate flip. Obviously, this means you will be spending more time and money on the project. However, if you planned and budgeted correctly before getting to this point in the venture, you will have taken all of this into account. There are a few areas that are exclusive to the total gut, as you'll see in the following sections.

Demolition

As with the intermediate flip, demolition is virtually the first physical thing you'll do to the building. The main difference in a total gut is there's a lot more of it to do. Irrespective of whether you're totally tearing the existing structure down to the ground or just gutting the entire interior and leaving the four walls in place, the sheer volume of work involved in the total gut means that your demo will also be much broader in scope. In some extreme cases, you'll even be demolishing the foundation and literally going right down to the ground. If your planned design and construction require a totally new foundation as the best way to succeed in your project, that's the way to go.

One area where a totally new foundation is a must is if your new construction is going to be on the same footprint, but add vertical mass. This assumes that the existing foundation is not sufficient to support the additional weight. Check with a structural engineer to be certain. If you're going from a single-story ranch or cottage to a two-story home, for example, you must first be certain that the foundation will support that additional weight. Likely, if it was engineered a number of years ago for just the single story; it will not adequately handle the additional mass. Thus, you will have to do a whole new foundation anyway. So, unless your engineer assures you that the existing foundation will take the added mass and weight, figure in a new foundation.

Framing

Once you have finished your demolition and, assuming it was necessary, finished your new foundation, you can proceed through the framing stage of construction. This procedure is basically the same as in an intermediate flip, just more comprehensive. Whether your total gut involved the demolition of the original structure or just the complete gutting of the interior will govern the amount of framing you will do, but in either case, if you are adding area on the ground floor, you will have additional framing work to do.

While I'm on the subject, as far as interior walls go, in many warmer sections of the country, basements are the exception rather than the rule, and "cellar" refers to a place to store wine. However, in parts of the country where basements are the norm, it is not uncommon to have one or two rooms in this area of the house. They are commonly used for family or rec rooms, workshops, offices, or extra bedrooms. As you would expect in such a configuration, there will be the appropriate interior framing to delineate the bounds of each of these rooms.

Should you go above a ground floor, once the first floor's walls are in, the floor joists will have to be laid across the headers at the top of the first floor's framing, and then the framing for the upper floor will then extend upward from that point.

Regardless of whether your project is a single-story or two-story home, the process from here on is the same as that of the intermediate flip, except that you'll be doing more of the same to get this part completed.

Roofing

The same is true with the roof. If you've retained the outer shell of the structure, your decision on roofing will be dictated by its age, condition, and in some cases, style. If you've completely razed the original structure, then it's obvious—you'll be going with a completely new roof.

Depending upon your plans, you might change the style of the roof. Where there may have been a traditional pitched roof covered with composition shingles, you may now go with a mansard, and cover it in cedar shakes. In areas that have had increasing risk of wildfire in recent years, such as parts of the western United States, perhaps you'll find yourself substituting concrete shingles that resemble cedar shakes, or, should the architectural style warrant, even going with a Spanish-style tile roof.

Finishing up

Once you have physically enclosed the shell of the structure, while the interior installation of systems is proceeding, on the exterior, you can finish the outer wall surface. You already nailed up the sheeting across the framing. Now you can proceed with the siding or shingling, whichever you plan to have as the exterior covering for the walls.

Another item that is usually exclusive to a total gut is the chimney. While doing a total gut doesn't require a new chimney unless you completely raze the original structure, this type of project does offer the opportunity to change the location, size, and style of chimney along with the house itself. If the new fireplace you're

Moneysaver

Save money on new chimneys by combining a manufactured firebox, stainless steel chimney, and a brick or stone veneer.

planning for the great room is to be river rock, for example, why go with a brick chimney? If you're doing a cast-iron wood stove for a den, perhaps you'll have at least the upper portion, if not the entire chimney, in metal. You may even have retained the fireplace and chimney, while tearing down most of the house, but then decide that you don't care for red brick. It might be possible to place a stone veneer over the brick to give your fireplace and chimney a new look.

The larger the amount of floor area that is involved in your total gut, the more likely it is that you may find yourself mixing the type of flooring you use in the finished project. Once the subfloor is installed in the structure, you may decide to have most of the more heavily used areas done in hardwood, with wall-to-wall carpet in such places as the master suite. The direction you go with flooring will depend on a combination of your own taste and budget, coupled with what is popular at the time you do your project, as well as the market you are trying to appeal to. However, as with the intermediate flip, don't install any carpet until after you've finished the painting and other interior work.

Now that your total gut is enclosed, exterior walls and roof complete, and windows hung, you can proceed as with an intermediate flip. First install the operating systems of the house: plumbing, electrical, and heating/air conditioning. Once these are in, with all electrical outlets and pipe stubs for faucets and spigots installed, you can nail up and tape the sheetrock.

From here continue on with painting, as well as any design details such as half-walls, fireplaces, and so on. Then do your cabinets, counters, and flooring, followed by any wallpapering you have planned. Next will come finishing details such as moldings and trim.

Yard and exterior

I mentioned a few pages ago that there are some areas that are exclusive to the total gut. This is not to say someone couldn't include them in an intermediate flip, but it would be unusual due to the extra time and expense required to do so. I briefly dealt with the subject of patios, decks, and other outside extras in the discussion of schedules for intermediate flips. It is here, on the total gut, that you can get more deeply involved in such additions.

The larger the house, the more opportunity you have to add decks and patio areas. Additionally, you will have more of a chance to have interesting architectural extras that make sense in the scope of a total gut, such as a pergola or portico over an entryway, back yard gazebo, pool, hot tub, exercise room, tennis court, or sport court.

In some cases, given enough room in the yard, the addition of a small second building may be desirable. This might serve as a guest unit, an office, an artist's studio, or some combination of these. How involved you get with something like this depends on what your plans and budget allow for, and what price point in the market you are aiming for.

Lawn and garden

Having finished with the construction, you can devote your attention to the walks and driveways, as well as the gardens and lawn. If you think back to the demo stage of this project, you may remember that one of the items you looked at in the land-scaping part of the work was how many, if any, of the existing plantings and/or trees you were going to save. Those you planned to save were given that status because they looked too nice or colorful to discard just for the sake of discarding, or, in the case of trees, hedges, or things such as rose bushes, were so

 Moneysaver

Some nurseries will give discounts for large multiple purchases.

mature that replacing them with something as pleasing to the eye would have been either impossible or too expensive.

What you do for a lawn will depend in large part on what existed when you started the project and what you managed to keep during demolition and construction. If you had a lawn that was well maintained when you purchased the property, it is likely that you took steps to protect and maintain as much of the existing lawn as possible, so now you will have minimal extra expense to have an attractive lawn.

If, however, the lawn was looking pretty ratty to begin with, or demo and construction involved so much that there was no way to really protect what was there, it is likely that you'll be installing a new lawn. In this case, the best way to go is to have new sod installed. It doesn't take very long, and because it looks lush from the start, it's a great way to attract potential buyers to your finished product. You may also want to include a new irrigation system, which I'll discuss in the next section. It protects your investment in the new sod and is an additional selling point to potential buyers.

It is at this stage that you will have consulted a landscaping architect, at least for recommendations on what plants or shrubs to add and where. It's usually best to have a basic background of green accented with clusters of color, but this is a matter of personal taste. There is nothing wrong with a garden plan that concentrates on heavy use of colorful flowers, accented by the occasional green bush or two.

I prefer roses for a variety of color, with some accenting provided by a single color of another blooming plant, such as lavender. It's relatively easy to grow, takes very little maintenance other than water, and comes in a variety of different versions and shades.

 Watch Out!

Don't roll out the new sod before first preparing the ground by rototilling it and adding fertilizer.

Whatever you do in the front of the house contributes to the home's curb appeal. In the other areas of the yard, extras are the frosting on the cake, so to speak, that complete the appealing appearance that you have given your project so that buyers will want to purchase it.

Irrigation systems

It is definitely a selling point if there is some form of irrigation system already installed to keep the plants and lawn alive and well. It doesn't have to be very elaborate. It can be something as simple as a system that is manually operated whenever the homeowner wants to turn it on and off. It can be a single type of piped system, or a combination of materials.

In the latter case, you may have some areas that require more water, such as a lawn where you use a full piped and sprinklered system, while other flower beds may be watered by a drip irrigation system. The drip portion will handle the needs of the plants and save on the volume of water used. Installation of a drip irrigation system is so simple that any changes required by the buyer as plants and flowers are added or moved can be done with little or no expertise. It's basically cutting and connecting lengths of tubing and inserting drip heads where the person wants to direct the water.

If you want something a little more elaborate, you can connect the irrigation system to a timer that can be set to different on-off sequences so you can water different areas at different times. For a typical home, this is not terribly expensive, but is an attractive extra. However, it is not by any means an absolute "must-have" requirement. I have seen homes for sale both with and without sprinkler systems, and in each case the home sold with little regard to whether or not there was a sprinkler system for the yard.

 Moneysaver

If installing yard irrigation, drip systems are less expensive than fully piped systems, and they save water.

Watch Out!

If you buy large trees, be sure to factor in the additional expense of needing a crane to lift and move the tree, as well as machinery to dig the hole required to fit each tree. Such costs can equal the cost of the tree.

Trees

Adding one or two (or more) strategically placed trees enhances the overall appearance of a lot. They can be done as a decorative cluster or as individual trees delineating boundary points of the lot. While trees can be purchased at nearly their full size, this will also have a direct impact on your budget. The larger the tree, the more it will cost you.

For example, if you were to buy a few small saplings, they might run a few hundred dollars apiece. On the other extreme, the same species of tree in a mature state will likely cost thousands of dollars per tree. A few examples of tree costs are shown in the following table.

Size	Trunk Thickness	Height at Purchase	Cost per Tree
5 gallon	Under 1 inch	Under 5 feet	$40-$50
15 gallon	2 inches	8-15 feet	$100-$150
24-inch boxed	2-3 inches	15-18 feet	$350-$450
36-inch boxed	4-6 inches	15-22 feet	$1,000-$2,000

(These figures are for common garden-variety trees, not your more exotic varieties that can be found through some nurseries. For example, anything beyond the basic version of Japanese Maple will run at least $100 for a 5-gallon container, $200 to $300 for a 15-gallon, and $500 to $1,000 for a 24-inch box.)

Another aspect to consider regarding existing trees is whether the existing tree is unique or visually interesting enough to want

Watch Out!

The compression of the ground from trucks, materials, and traffic can damage the root structure of a tree even if the tree itself has been protected.

to "work around" it, or, in some cases, even include it in the structure. The latter is sometimes done where a deck is built encircling the trunk of the tree, thus preserving both its beauty and shade, not to mention its value.

In some cases, even if the tree is not close to the structure, you'll want to keep the tree because it is so beautifully gnarled or twisted that there would be no way to replace it regardless of the amount you'd be willing to spend. A good example of this is an oak tree, variously estimated at 200 to 300 years of age, that stood near a home on which a client of mine did a total gut. The tree was so huge and so beautifully twisted and spread that he took special pains to preserve it. He even went to the extreme of adding in steel cables to provide support to a couple of large limbs to lessen the strain they placed upon the trunk, thus making it more likely the limbs could be preserved. Today the tree stands outside a nearly all-glass breakfast room off the finished flip's kitchen. However, this particular house is a unique one, and was a multi-million dollar house at its completion.

Hardscape

Other outside features to consider are the walks and driveway, frequently referred to as the hardscape. If the property you started with has walks and a driveway that are functional, look good, and are in good condition, you may have decided not to change them. However, with the wide variety in design and materials available today for these areas, if it fits within your budget, you might consider changing one or both of these items to go along with your new building. The basic is concrete, and it can be done in as many different ways as you can imagine. You can have a basic unadorned concrete sidewalk and driveway, or add attractive accents to the finished product with decorative wood strips placed geometrically across the paving or inserts of colorful tile or individual pieces of stone every so often.

From concrete you can move through a wide array of stone surfaces, ranging from cobblestone to fieldstone, from Arizona flagstone to Connecticut bluestone. The possible colors are too many to mention, but it is safe to say that if you can conceive of a color for your stone, it can probably be found. Other surfaces include brick or gravel, again in a large choice of colors. Some flips will have a combination of surfaces, one for the driveway and a different one for the walkway. This is again a matter of personal preference. You may also choose to increase visual appeal by planting narrow rows of grass or ground cover between the stones or bricks in your paved area. All of this comes under the category of curb appeal. The area is functional, but it also attracts the potential buyer by its appearance because it is a little bit different than the norm.

Another way to increase the visual interest in the driveway and sidewalks is to combine two or more materials used in the work. Sometimes, for example an outer border area of the paved area will be done in concrete, while the interior section will be completed with stones or gravel, or even planted in grass or some other ground cover. I know of some instances where the interior "panel" was made in a random curving pattern in a contrasting dark stone material so that it took on the appearance of a stream in the driveway. Treatments such as these will not appreciably increase your cost, and they will add a lot in terms of appeal to potential buyers. However, before you decide to do something like this, compare the expense to a "plain" driveway or walk.

Unexpected problems

One of the things I have stressed throughout this book is the importance of planning. There is a reason for this. Simply put, good planning lessens the likelihood that you'll have problems as you go along. However, even in the best-planned ventures sometimes things go wrong. It is just a fact of life. It is also one of the primary reasons why there is always risk to doing a flip. Remember, this book is a guide to flipping. It is *not* a guarantee that every time you attempt one everything will go forward without a hitch, making you rich and successful. During the course of a flip, problems can suddenly arise that may delay the projected time for you to finish the flip, or cause you to spend more money than originally planned.

Delays mean extra time, and, assuming the bank is financing you, extra time means extra costs, which can erode your projected profit. Extra expenditures to cure problems will have the same effect on your bottom line. All of this is the reason why, back in Chapter 5, I suggested including a "contingency expense" of 10 percent in the budget. The idea is that it should, in most cases, cover the costs associated with any unexpected problems that arise, and allow you to finish your venture more or less on budget and with most of the profit you'd expected.

One of the most common issues that can arise is a delay in permits. Even though you discussed your plans in general with the appropriate authorities early on (see Chapter 7), they would not have given you the actual permits necessary to begin work until they actually saw the formal plans. Perhaps while the plans were being completed a new ordinance or two was passed by the local governing entity. Because of this, you had to go back and redraw plans, thus delaying your permits. Maybe at the public hearings leading up to final permit approval the local community raised an objection that necessitated you and your architect having to go back and make changes in your designs and plans. Again, you were delayed in getting started.

Another common source of problems occurs during work. Materials ordered well in advance sometimes don't arrive on

 Bright Idea

To be on the safe side, plan on problems of some kind occurring—and if they don't, count yourself as fortunate!

time. Maybe the manufacturer underestimated the demand for your windows, or the source of your cabinets had an unexpected lag in production due to a fire at a production plant or a workers' strike. Whatever the reason, you've now got some of your materials on back order. It may be only a few days, or it could be months. The longer the delay, the more costly it can be for you, and not only in terms of extra interest to the lender financing you. You could also be affected by the delay by a change in market conditions causing lower prices for finished homes when you finally get to market your completed venture.

Another way this could cost you more money is if you have to locate replacement material from another source. The replacements could cost extra money, either because they are a different brand, from a different supplier, or due to market conditions for that particular type of material at the time that you have this problem arise.

Dealing with this problem differs from situation to situation. Where possible, you can work around the delay in materials delivery by moving up some other part of the work on your schedule. But at some point you may have to stop work while you wait for the missing material to arrive.

Some of your local workers may get sick. This always seems to happen just when it's their time to handle a specific phase of the project. You can solve this problem by hiring replacements. It is something you'll have to decide at the time it happens.

Hopefully, your contingency expense will cover these added costs. Ideally, you'll be able to meet whatever challenge arises, pay the extra cost from your budgeted contingency funds, and still have a bit of that left over when you finish the project so it will drop to the bottom line and increase your profit a bit. But, as I've said, there is no guarantee.

Progress inspections

These are exactly what the name implies. As you proceed through the construction process, you will have inspections performed. Some, in the case of work by subcontractors, you or your general contractor will do just to be sure that the work you're paying for is done correctly before you disburse any funds. Other inspections are usually performed by the local permitting authority through the office of the building inspector.

These serve two purposes. First, they ensure that applicable codes are being adhered to in the construction performed. Second, in most jurisdictions, they serve to renew the overall building permit for another period of time. The most common timing is a six-month period for the building permit. Every time a new inspection is made by the building inspector, the permit is renewed or extended for another six months. Some of these are final inspections of the individual components of the project. For example, the electrical system will be "finaled," as will the heating and plumbing systems.

Once construction is completed, a final inspection is made by the local building inspector and you're ready to put the completed project on the market. Be sure to carefully schedule the inspections, because they can delay work for a number of days, depending on the pre-existing schedule of the local inspectors.

Just the facts

- Start by establishing a work schedule.
- Order materials well in advance. Where necessary, build in a little extra time to avoid delays from late delivery.
- You can save time and money by simultaneously roofing the house and installing the operating systems—plumbing, electrical, and HVAC—of the structure.
- Expect to have problems and delays crop up. If you're ready for them, they may not cause as much trouble as they would otherwise.
- Schedule your inspections as far in advance as possible to avoid unexpected delays caused by the inspector's overall schedule.

PART V

Taking It to the Bank

GET THE SCOOP ON...
Pricing the property ▪ Your Realtor's knowledge
of the market ▪ Electronic marketing techniques
▪ Other marketing options

Selling Your Gem

There are a couple of different ways to handle the marketing and sale of your finished venture. You can hire a Realtor and have him or her oversee the process. It's not a requirement, but if you go this route, it is very likely that the Realtor you hire will be the same one who helped you locate the property to begin with. The only reason you may go with another agent is that something didn't quite work between you and the Realtor as you proceeded through the purchase process. Or you may want to save yourself the commission and go it alone. This latter method, referred to as a FSBO, or For Sale By Owner, will be discussed in the next chapter.

The reasons for engaging a Realtor to sell your completed gem are based on that individual's experience and expertise. The experience of the Realtor is obvious. It speaks for itself. Unless the person is a freshly minted agent, he or she will have years of experience in listing, marketing, and selling homes in the area where your project is located, and will be familiar with all the nuances that that particular market requires to be successful.

Moneysaver

Don't just accept the commission rate your Realtor quotes you. Negotiate. Commissions are not fixed, but fully negotiable. There are even "cut-rate" Realtors who are dramatically cheaper, but remember—in such cases, you get what you pay for.

Their expertise will be composed of knowledge of proper pricing, market conditions, assembling the proper marketing program for your property, use of their own marketing network as part of the marketing of your property, and addressing the ever-expanding issues of disclosure.

Pricing expertise

One of the most difficult parts of selling real estate is pricing properties properly. No matter how tempting it may be to seek the highest possible amount, you don't want to overprice and have the property just sit on the market unsold. Worse, if you overprice, you'll eventually be forced to lower the price to reflect the property's real value, but the market will have moved on, likely causing your gem to remain unsold. Again, you'll lower your price and chase the market downward until the price you finally receive will be less than you could have received had you only priced it sensibly to begin with.

On the other hand, you don't want to price a property too low, get an immediate sale, and then realize that you left thousands of dollars literally sitting on the table. Unfortunately, there is no exact science to pricing a house. The numbers of bedrooms or baths, how many decks you may have, or the size of the living space or lot do not automatically compute to a specific set of numbers for your price.

With the possible exception of the homes in a brand-new subdivision, every house is different from every other house, even if they are side by side, and any number of factors can affect the amount of money that they will command on the open market.

Virtually every Realtor has her own method of pricing a house to sell, but most methods have many common factors. The most common is looking carefully at the prices that comparable homes in the immediate area have received in recent months, and how long it took to sell each of those homes. Obviously, if your flip is a four-bedroom, two-and-a-half-bath, two-story, garrison-style, wood-frame home with 2,000 square feet of living area, and the six other homes in the immediate area that match that size, number of bedrooms and baths, and style have all sold for between $350,000 and $389,000, you shouldn't price yours for $425,000 and expect it to sell.

Absorption rate

Another factor to consider that is directly related to where you price your property is the *absorption rate* on the market. That is the rate at which the market will absorb, or sell, all the homes in a particular price range, or, in the broader market analysis, all the homes on the market at any given time, regardless of price. It is a calculation that your Realtor can make very easily and, in a matter of moments, show you.

By *absorption,* I mean how long it will take to sell all the homes on the market. If the market is slowing down or it's already a buyers' market, it usually takes longer for the market to absorb any inventory it has at any given time. Your property is just "one more on the pile." Obviously, you are not going to want to hinder the chances of your home being among the first the market absorbs. So, when your Realtor suggests a price for your home based on recent comps, it would be a good idea to follow his or her advice. (*Comps* is short for *comparables*, those similar properties to your flip in the same geographical area that either have recently sold or are currently on the market.)

When your Realtor goes over the comps with you, he or she will not only discuss all the comps that have recently sold, but also other comps of a similar nature that are currently on the market and their prices. Additionally, your Realtor will point out any homes of that type of comp that may have failed to sell and tell you why they didn't sell. If you have any questions about any of these homes, your Realtor may even take you around to see as many of them as is possible, at least insofar as those on the market are concerned.

CAMO

A number of leading Realtors have also added another step in the pricing process. Just before your home goes on the market, the Realtor will have a number of other agents who specialize in that particular area come in and look at the house to get their opinions of what the price should be. Called a CAMO, the process involves four to six agents coming through the house at a particular time, looking at all the details, and then individually writing their estimate of price on the back of their card and giving it to your agent. After everyone has left, your agent sits down with you and compares all these recommended prices. Usually, this process produces a common price or price range and simultaneously provides you and your agent with a better sense of what the market may think of value. Again, it is no guarantee of a correct price, but it is an indicator of where your price should be.

It is worth noting one other thing about pricing a home. Irrespective of how much information your Realtor provides you in regard to pricing your home, unless you have an agreement whereby your Realtor specifically will make the decision for you, the ultimate decision on price is yours to make. Pick your price, but remember: If you believe in that Realtor enough to have hired him or her to sell your property, take his or her recommendations on pricing into account before you choose a number. The Realtor's job is to help you get the best possible price for your property in the least amount of time.

Market knowledge

Market knowledge goes hand in hand with pricing strategy, and it's one of the reasons to pay attention to your Realtor when he or she recommends a price range for your property. Based on the Realtor's expertise and knowledge of exactly what is happening at any particular time in the market, he or she is best positioned to make a pricing recommendation. If interest rates are moving—up or down—the Realtor will be very much aware of it because such a trend affects virtually all of his or her business.

Anytime one of the Realtor's buyers makes an offer on a property, interest rates will have an effect on the deal. If the Realtor represents a seller, and that includes you, the rates of interest are going to have an effect on how many buyers will likely qualify for a mortgage to be able to purchase the property in question. Additionally, if the Realtor works like I do, he or she will have regular contact with one or two mortgage brokers to maintain a current knowledge level of the interest rates on the market at any given time, as well as the trend that they are showing.

Your Realtor is also likely to know if any particular type of property is in or out of favor on the market at a particular time. Sometimes, larger homes with family rooms are in fashion; other times they may be less in favor. Perhaps a certain area has fallen from favor due to the quality of its schools or increased noise from a nearby freeway. Your Realtor will be aware of these factors and can advise you about them. Because of his or her constant activity in the market, both for clients and for the need to remain up to date on market conditions, your agent will know more quickly of such changes in buyers' tastes in a market at any specific time.

In some areas, a sudden decision by the leading employer to increase or reduce the size of its local operations can be a major factor in market conditions. This would include things like plant additions or closures. The downsizing of a regional base by one or more of the major airline companies, due to such things as security or fuel cost issues, can also have an effect on the local real estate market.

Some other items that a knowledgeable agent will be aware of include any local government decisions regarding new ordinances or bond issues. For example, if the local town government where your project is has announced plans to put a bond

Watch Out!

Potential competition from other new projects that are likely to come to market at or near the same time as yours may have a definite damping effect on the price you receive for your venture. If your agent is aware of such competitive forces, he or she can advise you accordingly.

issue on this fall's ballot to underwrite expansion of the high school's science labs, gymnasium, and adjoining athletic field, it could have the effect of making the area more desirable for families with children in or approaching high school age. This would presumably improve the market for homes in the area.

If your project's locale has the misfortune of being in proximity to a creek that floods almost every year, but the federal government has just passed a bill to improve flood prevention resources, it should make your project more inviting to potential buyers.

These are just a few examples of how your agent's market knowledge can be helpful. It is very likely that your agent's market knowledge will extend far beyond these few examples, but they serve as a good reason to pay attention when your agent recommends a certain pricing level to you.

Property marketing expertise

The expertise your Realtor has in marketing a property is one gained through his long experience doing exactly that. He or she knows what helps sell a house and what can deter buyers from choosing your project as their next home. A Realtor's knowledge is constantly evolving as he or she handles more properties in more varied market conditions and becomes familiar and adept at the use of more varied marketing methods in his or her marketing activity. Simply put, your Realtor knows what will or won't work in the marketing of a property such as yours.

Traditionally, the items involved in a marketing plan for a home included the Multiple Listing System (MLS), print advertisements, flyers, and open houses, both public and agents only. While these things still are heavily featured in most property marketing programs, the advent of the computer and the Internet have dramatically changed their place in a marketing plan, and in home marketing methods overall.

Electronic marketing

Since the advent of the Web and e-mail have had such an effect on home marketing, let's examine that aspect of marketing your project first. We will look at the traditional marketing methods afterward. According to the National Association of Realtors (NAR), the first thing most home buyers do when they start looking for a property is to log on to the Web. The NAR's most recent statistics indicate that at least 74 percent of all buyers pick up a computer mouse before picking up the phone, even if they already know which Realtor they will use. That number is increasing annually, and by the time you read this, will likely have passed 80 percent.

Originally, as Realtors became familiar with the Web, most properties were found on the Web sites of the various real estate firms. As time passed, local boards of Realtors added Web accessibility to their MLSs. While this was happening, individual Realtors began to create their own Web sites to promote both themselves and their listings. (Mine is www.peterandjanerichmond.com.)

As if that weren't enough, an increasing number of agents began creating multiple Web sites, with those beyond their principal Web site being targeted at a specific market, or for general promotion of themselves in a particular market segment. Some, myself included, purchased multiple Internet domain names.

 Bright Idea

Make sure the Realtor representing you is technologically savvy and someone who will utilize the Internet as a place to show off your home to potential buyers. Ideally, the agent will use multiple Web sites.

Some of these multiple domains actually had separate sites created, while others automatically bounced to the main Web site of the individual Realtor. I use www.endyourrent.com, one of nearly a dozen domains I own, to attract first-time buyers to my site and the listings I currently have for sale.

Carrying this use of the Internet two steps further, many leading agents get expanded exposure for their listed properties by placing them with Realtor.com, and by the creation of a custom Web site solely for the individual property. Realtor.com is the Web site of the National Association of Realtors and the largest real estate Web site in the world. Any Realtor placing his listing on Realtor.com can, for a relatively small fee, have his or her placement "enhanced" on that site. This enhancement then allows the Realtor's property listings to be picked up by multiple other sites on the Web across the country, such as local newspapers, national search engine real estate pages, and radio or TV stations' Web sites. It is partly through this vehicle that I can honestly tell a potential seller of mine that his or her property will be placed on at least 86 separate Web sites across the nation. Some of these sites are part of major media outlets such as the *New York Times* or AOL. Others are merely local town newspapers or TV stations' Web sites that have arrangements with Realtor.com to access its site.

Custom Web site creation came into being around the year 2000. The concept is simple: Each property has its own Web site created for its marketing by the listing Realtor. Not all Realtors use this tool, but if your Realtor is on top of the market, it is likely he or she will be using this tool. The sites vary, but all have one thing in common. The Web address, or URL, will always be www.*whateverthepropertyaddressis*.com. For example, if your property is at 250 Shady Lane, the custom Web site would be www.250shadylane.com.

Another nice feature of having your property featured on the Web is that anyone, as well as your agent, can view the property and its relevant information even while away from their

Bright Idea

Many MLSs allow users of their systems to e-mail listings from the system to anyone they choose. An agent who happens to see your project at a brokers' open house can immediately go to the MLS Web site and e-mail details of that listing to a client who might have an interest in your property.

home or office. If they have a laptop computer with wireless technology, they can look at your project while sitting in gridlock traffic on the freeway, waiting for a plane, or between courses at their favorite restaurant.

Usually, these sites are created for the duration of the time the particular property is on the market. Once the property has sold and closed, or shortly thereafter, they are usually removed from the Web. Some agents—and I am one of them—leave these custom sites up for a few months after the sale has closed as a marketing tool for other potential clients. They can demonstrate exactly how a custom Web site will work for that potential client's property.

Apart from the Internet, there are other electronic marketing techniques that an up-to-date Realtor will use to market your property. E-mail has become the best way of directly communicating with anyone, agent or potential buyer, who may have an interest in a particular property. With just a few key strokes, the agent can send information about any property to anyone seeking the information. He can electronically attach pictures, floor plans, or disclosure documents to that same recipient. He can even e-mail virtual tours of the property, an item I'll talk about in the next section. In fact, any item that can be reduced to documentary form can be transmitted by e-mail to the potential buyer or agent.

Virtual tours

As technology has continued to develop, another marketing tool has been created: the virtual tour. Designed to help market properties from a distance, it enables the viewer to "tour" the property electronically without ever having to set foot in the actual building. Generally, it encompasses a video or still photos of the different rooms and other features of the house, sometimes along with commentary or script that describes each room being viewed at a given moment on the tour. These tours can be e-mailed, placed on Web sites, or burned onto CDs or DVDs for distribution to potential buyers and their agents. The better virtual tours make it seem almost as though you're walking through the actual property!

Just as flyers and photos are designed to give potential buyers and agents a positive impression of the property, so too are virtual tours intended to leave a positive taste in the mouths of the same people. They also expand on the potential impact that a single picture can leave with its viewers.

Traditional marketing

This is the marketing format used by most Realtors for all of their listings. While some of the techniques have changed with time and technology, the methodology has not. However, better agents make better use of it than others.

The first item is the MLS, or Multiple Listing System, which I've already discussed. This is the system assembled and run by an agent's local Board of Realtors. It allows its members to list any property they currently have for sale, along with the important details of the property, how to get to see it, and directions to its location. The listing will also usually notify agents when open houses and brokers' tours are to be held. As I noted previously, many of today's MLSs have Web accessibility included for their listings.

The balance of traditional marketing combines print marketing and open houses. Print marketing uses both newspaper and magazine advertising that features the house and announces dates of public open houses. The value of the property, coupled with the target market, will be factors in determining how prominent an ad will be. Real estate ads can and do run the gamut from tiny copy-only listings in the local newspaper's classified section to full-page color ads in high-end publications such as *The Robb Report, Du Pont Registry,* and *Pinnacle.*

Frequency of the ads is another part of the marketing plan your Realtor will devise for the property. Ads announcing the open houses will obviously only run the week or weekend of the actual open house, while separate ads describing the property in more detail will likely run at least once a week for the first few weeks, and then, if the property is still unsold, every other week, usually between the weeks that open houses are held.

> **❝**When I'm doing a flip, I always go to open houses in the neighborhood to see what is selling and to talk with Realtors to get hints.**❞**
>
> —Robert, experienced flipper

Your agent may also create and distribute flyers or brochures showing the property to its best advantage. These should have some information on the property's highlights as well as one or more good color photos of the house. Depending on the price point of the property, its special features, and the format the agent prefers to use, it will likely be one or two pages. In the case of higher-end properties, or those of unique design and detail, the agent may decide to create a three- or four-page brochure to hand out to prospective buyers and their agents.

The distribution of flyers even has its own variations, depending on the agent and the location of the property. With few exceptions, the agent will have a "For Sale" sign erected on the property as soon as it is ready for marketing. In some cases, a flyer box will also be attached to the signpost that offers flyers to potential buyers. These flyers provide information to people who either couldn't get to an open house when it was held, or just happen to be passing the house by chance, see it, and are interested enough to want more information before calling the Realtor.

Bright Idea

The office of the real estate brokerage your agent is affiliated with will also display flyers about your property. These are usually hanging in the office's window in a display case inside the brokerage for the availability of anyone passing by the office.

Sometimes, for a higher-end property, the agent will send out invitations to the surrounding neighborhood to attend the first open house. These invitations will be custom created and usually include a brief sample of the information contained in the flyer. The theory behind getting neighbors into the open houses is that, in many cases, they may have had friends or co-workers as guests at their homes and had those people tell them that they were so impressed with the neighborhood that they should be contacted if any home became available in the area. What better way to get a potential buyer than to have someone who has already decided that they love the area where you have just completed your venture?

Realtor's network

Another facet of a well-planned marketing campaign is the Realtor's personal network. This is exactly what it says it is. As with any industry, after one of its practitioners has been involved for some time, that person develops a pretty good network of other agents with whom he or she has worked or discussed properties during that time span. The agent becomes comfortable with these various agents, and may even have a regular networking meeting with them every week or two. When these meetings are held, or sometimes even in advance of them, a good agent will notify other members in his network that he or she has a new listing coming to market in the near future. At that time, the agent will also provide details and, if possible, the price of the property to his or her network colleagues. This is just one more way of getting the news around about your house to as many people as possible. Also, it is not uncommon for another network member to have a client already looking for just the type of property that your project happens to be. When that happens, you may have a buyer before your property is even officially put on the market.

Another benefit of the network is that often agents are members of different networking groups. This means that one or more members of your agent's network may, in turn, be members of other networks. If so, they will spread the information given them about your house to their other networks, thus broadening the audience learning of your property.

Disclosure

Another part of marketing a property may not seem like actual marketing, but it is every bit as important as any ad or flyer that the agent may create. This is disclosure. While laws on the subject vary from state to state, there is one commonality: All states require that the seller and his agent reveal any defects, potential problems, or other issues negatively affecting the property that they are aware of. The days of *caveat emptor* (buyer beware) have long since passed when it comes to selling real estate.

Varying with the state, the disclosures you make on or about the property usually cover not only the property itself, but in many cases, the surrounding area as well. For example, if there is a great deal of noise from a nearby highway or other source, you should disclose this. If your venture lies near a landfill or other site that may not be pleasing to a future owner, it should be disclosed. Perhaps there is a cemetery about half a mile away, a river that has been known to flood after heavy rains, or a new commercial construction project has been announced a little over a mile away. All of these are examples of offsite items that should be disclosed to potential buyers. The reasons for disclosure are simple. In most cases, they are what the law requires, either by actual statute or as a result of a previous lawsuit on the subject.

Watch Out!

Failure to disclose what you know is negative or potentially negative about a property is a guaranteed way of being sued some time after you conclude the sale. If you disclose the issue, you avoid this problem.

From a purely marketing point of view, however, there is an equally good reason to disclose, and do it before you are in contract on the property. A good agent will prepare packages of your disclosures to provide to potential buyers who have expressed interest in the property once they have actually seen it. On the theory that these people may make you an offer, it gives these potential purchasers the opportunity to review all of your disclosures and learn of any issues, real or perceived, about the property, and then decide if they wish to make an offer.

You may ask what the difference is in doing this before or after they make an offer. The answer is simple: It is far better to eliminate any potential buyers from the process by letting them learn of any issues that would keep them from buying the house than to have them make an offer, have it accepted, and then drop out of the purchase upon learning of the issues in the disclosures. If they do so only after they have had an offer accepted while they are doing their due diligence, your property comes back on the market having lost all of its momentum in getting and holding the attention and interest of the buyers in the current market and their agents. Having this happen will make it that much harder to sell your property and only delay the process. A knowledgeable agent will avoid this by providing disclosure packets before the offer is even made, thus weeding out those unlikely to stay with a purchase through closing.

Although most items suitable for disclosure are pretty obvious, sometimes a seller is uncertain. Maybe he or she feels it may not really be an issue with the property, or it is one that depends on a buyer's perception of the subject, a perception that can be directed toward a desired conclusion by proper marketing information. I have always leaned toward a more cautious approach and recommend that you do as well. My feeling is that if it even occurs as a question of disclosure to you, then you should disclose it. If you do not, and it later crops up in a lawsuit, you can be certain that you will be asked, under oath, if you knew of this issue and considered disclosing it.

Just the facts

- Listen to your Realtor when pricing the property. The agent's an expert at the nuances involved and will base a price recommendation on a combination of market analysis and a knowledge of other factors affecting the market.

- Pay attention to your Realtor—he or she acquired knowledge through a great deal of experience in many areas affecting the market, including demographics, interest rates, government actions, and the pace of the market.

- Today more and more real estate is sold using technology. This includes the Internet, e-mail, and virtual tours of properties.

- Traditional marketing methods—print, flyers, and open houses—still have their place in selling a house.

- Seller's disclosures are important; providing them to prospective buyers can both eliminate tentative buyers and alleviate for the seller the aggravation of future lawsuits from distressed buyers.

GET THE SCOOP ON...
Doing it yourself: FSBO ▪ Using your network to
get the word out ▪ Staging the home's interior ▪
Staging the yard

For Sale by Owner

hapter 15 examined the benefits of using a Realtor to market your finished property. While I think I thoroughly covered the reasons for my preference for using a Realtor, some people feel that they'd do just as thorough a job marketing and selling the finished property themselves. In a few cases, they may be right. However, these relatively few situations are usually in cases where the flippers have done a number of property sales themselves in the past and have gained the experience and knowledge of the ins and outs of doing a sale by themselves. I am not implying that a first-time or second-time seller can't successfully sell a property without an agent. However, I am stressing that the most successful sellers who do it themselves are most frequently those with experience.

Doing a FSBO

The term used for selling a property by yourself is For Sale by Owner. It is more commonly referred to by its initials, FSBO (pronounced "fizz-bo"). It is everything that such an undertaking implies by the name. The owner handles all the details of marketing, selling, and closing the property. All the aspects of a complete marketing campaign to get the property sold, and for as much money as possible, that I discussed in Chapter 15 apply in the case of a FSBO. The only difference is that you have to take care of these details instead of relying on your Realtor and his or her staff to do so.

All the photos of your gem will be your responsibility to take, or have taken by a professional. It will be your responsibility to arrange to have the photos incorporated into all print marketing that you plan to do for the property—newspapers, magazines, flyers, open house notifications, just-listed cards—everything.

If you'll be using professional sketches or line drawings of the property as a marketing angle, it will be you, not your Realtor, contracting with the artist(s) and arranging for the sketches and drawings to be done and to the printer on time. Similarly, any photo reductions of architect's plans or floor plans to be included in whatever marketing material you assemble will have to be arranged by you.

Considering a virtual tour, and Web site exposure for the property? Once again, you are the one who'll have to arrange all the timing and uploading work for the photos to the Web and for the virtual tour to be created and then circulated to anyone and everyone you think might have an interest in receiving it.

While we're discussing the Web, ask yourself if you have the expertise to set up an entire Web site to display the property to its best advantage. If not, you'll have to pay a Webmaster to do this, and then, once he or she has completed the creation of the site, you'll have to pay someone, the Webmaster or another individual, to host the site. All of this extra expense will eat into your savings from doing a FSBO, as opposed to hiring a Realtor and letting him or her do the heavy lifting. Further, as noted in Chapter 15, it is highly likely that a top Realtor with lots of expertise in the use of technology, or the access to such expertise, will include your property on multiple Web sites. Every site on which you put your FSBO is likely to increase your costs. When a Realtor arranges it,

Moneysaver

If you are good with HTML, you can save hundreds of dollars by creating your own Web site for the property as part of your marketing strategy.

it's already included in the commission he or she is charging you—typically 6 percent of the selling price of the property.

If you are doing a FSBO, you have the additional issue of getting your property placed on the Multiple Listing System (MLS). An agent has no trouble with this. You may have at least some trouble. You usually can't get a property on the MLS by yourself if you are not a Realtor and a member of the local MLS or Board of Realtors. So how do you get around this? There are real estate brokerages that will, for a fee, upload your property onto the MLS. That is virtually *all* they will do. The only additional service they will perform relative to the MLS is to change the status of your property as you move through a sale, from active or for sale, to contingent or pending, to sold.

You will have to arrange to have open houses, either manning them yourself or paying someone to do so. Once you get this aspect out of the way, you have to make yourself available to show the house at any reasonable time buyers and their agents may want to see it, and "reasonable" can have a pretty wide range of definitions.

Let's assume, just to make matters a little more complicated, that the place where you and your venture are located is in a place that requires one or more pre-sale inspections by the local authorities. Normally, your Realtor arranges the inspections with the appropriate authorities, pays the fees, if any, and all you do is reimburse the agent his or her expense in that regard. Doing a FSBO, you have to go to the local city or county department, apply for the inspection, write the check, and make yourself available for the inspector when he or she comes by.

Once you do get an acceptable offer, and your would-be buyer commences the process of due diligence between having an offer accepted and closing, there will be a series of inspections by people hired by the buyer and the buyer's agent. You will have to make yourself available to the buyer's agent, or provide a loaner key, to open the house to the people doing these inspections, usually making yourself scarce during the process, and then showing up at their conclusion to close up the house again. This can be accomplished by the use of a lock box. These are available at most hardware stores.

One additional thing you'll probably have to take care of as well if you decide to do a FSBO is to pay the Realtor who represents the buyer, unless you're lucky and your ultimate buyer just happens to be house hunting without having attached herself to a Realtor when she first meets you and sees the house. So this means that, in most cases, you'll pay between 2 and 4 percent of the sales price, depending on the customary commission rates in your market, to the agent bringing you the buyer.

It is true that even when you add in the commission to the buyer's agent, all of the expenses you accumulated creating and implementing a marketing program to enable you to successfully do a FSBO will probably have cost you less than had you hired a Realtor in the first place. However, you have to ask yourself if the extra worries and aggravation to sell the property were worth the effort just to save a relatively small amount of cash. Now, I know I said earlier in this book that everything you don't have to spend money on increases your savings and, as a result, goes straight to the bottom line—your profit. However, there are some instances where expending a little extra cash can reduce your aggravation quotient, still leave you with a nice profit, and get the job done a lot more easily. It all depends, as I said at the start of this chapter, on how much experience in this end of the process you have.

For example, if you are very good with a camera and enjoy the creativity involved in getting really good marketing-quality photos, you can take all of the photos that a solid marketing campaign will require. If you have experience working in graphic arts or printing, you can definitely produce good-quality marketing materials such as flyers and brochures. Even if you're not gifted in these areas, you can bring your material to a print and copy shop such as Kinko's and probably get a satisfactory piece put together.

The same can be said for arranging advertisements in the print media and holding open houses. The former involves taking the time to arrange placement and ad setup or layout with the advertising department of the given publication. The latter merely requires a minimum level of sociability. If you're comfortable working with small groups, you can probably handle open houses reasonably well.

The biggest issue in doing any or all of this yourself, assuming you have the willingness and talent, is time. All of this takes time, and not a little bit. If you have the time and are willing to spend it, and feel comfortable handling all of the tasks involved, then go for it. However, if time is an issue, or if you don't have many of the skills needed, you may wish to rethink your FSBO plans.

Getting the word out

Just as a Realtor includes networking in the marketing of a property, you should also include this technique if you decide to FSBO your gem. If you sit down and think about it, you already have a network that can be helpful in getting your property sold. You probably know a few Realtors from past experience, or, at a minimum, from buying this property. Let them know about your property and when it will be available for sale, and for how much. It is likely that many local real estate brokerage offices will allow you to leave flyers at their offices for distribution to their agents and customers.

Perhaps you belong to a few local clubs or business associations, or the chamber of commerce. These are also network places to let people know that you have a house for sale, and a place to provide all of the necessary details.

Another part of your own network is the neighborhood where the property is located. Whether you live in the area or not, by its proximity to the property, this is a valuable part of

Bright Idea

You may want to go door to door to let the neighbors know when your house will be for sale, and for how much. Don't forget to leave them your contact information. It's also a good idea to invite neighbors to the open houses.

your marketing network, and should be fully involved. Include this area in any mailings you do or flyers you distribute.

Another way to not overlook part of your extended network is to use an old trick that many salespeople employ on beginning their sales careers. Sit down and make a list of everyone you know. Include friends and family as well as anyone with whom you come in regular contact, such as the postman, gardener, barber or hairstylist, butcher, auto mechanic, handyman, dry cleaner, shoe repair person, physician, or manicurist. You never know who will refer the buyer to you. It might not be a bad idea to include your clergyperson, especially if the market is slow. The local cop on the beat and your local town-elected representatives (at least those you supported) should be remembered. You get the point. Anyone you know should be notified and kept informed of the sale and marketing of your venture. The more people you tell, the better your chances of selling the property—and selling it for the amount you want.

You can buy a "For Sale" sign at any hardware or home improvement store. This can obviously be saved for future projects as well, should you find you have a talent for doing FSBOs.

Staging the property

Another thing that a Realtor can very easily handle, or that you can do yourself if you have some talent in this area, but one that you will pay for either way, is the process of staging your house for sale. A process that came into common use about seven or eight years ago, staging follows the theory that developers of entire subdivisions have used for decades. They make one of the homes in their new subdivisions the "model" home and have it professionally decorated with all of the latest furniture and color schemes, attractive trim items such as curtains and linens, and eye-catching floral arrangements and table settings.

The rationale for this is simple. The buyer comes into the house, sees the beautiful design setup of the décor, and thinks, "Wow! This house looks beautiful! I have to have it!" Forget the fact that it'll never look that good once the new owner takes possession. The owner *thinks* it will, so he or she buys it.

It's the same thing with staging. You get the house looking as good as it possibly can by hiring a stager, often an interior designer, and the buyers will immediately haul out their checkbooks, assuming the basic layout of the house meets their needs. Staging is adaptable to the particular property as well as the budget of the owner. It can be as simple as de-cluttering a house to a partial remodel and custom interior design. In fact, to a certain degree, the more involved staging jobs are not dissimilar from intermediate flips.

Another reason to use a stager is that most flips, when finished, are just empty houses. No matter how good a job you have done, the house is usually devoid of furniture and decorations. It is a simple fact of life—empty houses generally don't sell as quickly or for as much money as houses that are nicely furnished and decorated. Although there is really no way to tell, it is likely that the money it costs you to stage your venture will end up being less than the amount you will be able to add to your selling price because you staged the property.

In the case of a flip, regardless of the type of flip, the staging will be fairly involved. It will be more than rearranging furniture or de-cluttering the owner's possessions. It will involve bringing in furniture for at least three rooms; all the rooms would be better, but if your budget won't permit it, then three will be the minimum. It will also include such things as floral arrangements, artwork for the walls and shelves, filling bookshelves, and laying out the proper linen in the bedroom(s) and dinnerware for the dining area. It might even include details such as a small

Moneysaver

Staging has become so exact in its details that many stagers now include imitation stereos, televisions, and computers in the places they work on just to increase the air of authenticity in a home. They'd most likely prefer to use the real thing in this case, but, unlike furniture, home electronics are far easier to steal, so it's less expensive to use the imitations.

container of firewood and fireplace tools next to the fireplace, personal accessories in the bedroom and bath, and a small selection of clothing hanging in the closets to make the place have an even more genuine lived-in feel to it.

The staging process is simple. You have a stager or two come through the finished project and look it over. They analyze the floor plan and tell you what they will charge to do the job. Once you hire them, usually by contract for a specific period of time, they arrange for all of the furniture, artwork, and accessories to be delivered to the house, placing them in the appropriate locations. They will also arrive at the house on a regular basis to water any plants they have brought in, as well as change or replace any items of furniture or accessories that they feel should be changed. Once you have an accepted offer on the property, and all of the buyer's due diligence and financing contingencies have been released, the stagers will remove their things from the property, leaving it empty and available for the buyer's possessions after closing.

Outside the house

Whether you decide to stage outside of the house depends on your budget, the type of flip you have undertaken, and your own talents in this regard. Assuming the property either has attractive grounds, or you have included landscape improvements in your flip, it isn't likely that a stager handling the grounds will bring in new plantings. What a grounds stager will do is make the grounds around the house look more attractive and realistic to potential buyers. It also helps improve the home's curb appeal.

Some stagers handling the interior also handle staging the grounds. In other cases, you may prefer using the services of stagers specializing in the area outside the building to stage your yard. In either case, this involves bringing in yard furniture and accessories that would be likely to be found in the yard of such a home if someone were living there. These include yard and patio furniture, fire pits, barbeque sets and utensils, and potted plants. Even gardening tools and a garden hose on its own stand or movable rack may be included. Sometimes, a stager will incorporate children's toys or a sandbox. If there is a pool or hot tub, you may find pool accessories and furniture artfully arranged around the perimeter of the area. In higher-end homes with a cabana or changing area adjoining the pool, stagers will even stack towels, lay out containers of sunscreen, and have a few swimsuits neatly hung inside the changing areas.

If the home has a garage, many stagers will display a small group of tools on the interior wall of the structure, along with an assortment of automotive equipment and accessories for effect.

Just the facts

- A FSBO can be done to save money on Realtor commissions. Just be sure you're willing to spend the time necessary to try it.

- If you're technologically savvy, you can produce a workable Web site(s) for your property, and also utilize e-mail to get broad advertising coverage for your project.

- Even if you don't have graphic skills, a good print and copy shop such as Kinko's can create good marketing flyers for you.

- Staging sells houses. You'll get more for your house if it's staged than if it's empty.

- Don't forget about staging the outside of the house. Touches such as patio furniture, children's toys, and potted plants give the home a lived-in look that's attractive to potential buyers.

Chapter 17

It's Done! Final Considerations

ongratulations! You've completed your project! Whether this is your first or your hundredth flip, there is a certain indescribable feeling that will come over you once you reach this stage. Satisfaction? Pleasure? Everyone has their own description, and so will you. You've been through all the work and study and analysis necessary to get your project from its original inception as an idea to this point—actual physical completion. You're almost entitled to cash out and celebrate—almost. There are just a few relatively small details left, and then you're done. These few details can be referred to in a few words, all of which I'll explain in more detail in the following sections, to be certain that nothing gets forgotten during the celebration of the project being completed.

Closing documents

Closing documents are the documents that you sign as part of the official closing of the sale of the property. Whether it's at an escrow company or an attorney's office, you'll typically complete these documents as your part of the transaction as the seller of the property. Fortunately, there are generally fewer documents for the seller to sign than the buyer, so you'll have an easier time of it.

The documents you will sign include the following:

- The reconveyance from your lender who financed the project, assuming that the lender took a mortgage on the property as collateral for the loan. The reconveyance releases the bank's lien on the property, conveying it back to you so that you can sell it to the purchaser without any old liens against it. (You will actually not sign this; it will be completed by the lender and forwarded to the appropriate county recorder for recordation, removing you from the records as a liened debtor on the property.)

- The 1099-S form, which reports to the IRS the sale of the property. You'll be asked to insert your Social Security Number or Tax ID Number.

- A FIRPTA (Foreign Investment in Real Property Tax Act), and possibly a state equivalent of it, assuming that your state has income and/or capital gains tax. Some do, some don't. This document officially notifies the federal government that you've sold the property and how much you received so that they can collect any tax that is due on any profit you've realized from the transaction. If a foreign person sells property in the U.S., he or she is subject to a possible withholding of 10 percent of the sales price. Check out www.irs.gov and search FIRPTA for info.

- A HUD-1 Settlement Statement is the estimated closing statement of costs and receipts related to the closing of the sale. It includes the money you'll receive for the sale of the property, any payments you owe on the property, as well as the payoff of any financing on the property. Any prorated property tax, as well as any locally imposed resale taxes, will also be accounted for on this document.

▪ The deed. You sign the deed to officially pass your interest in the property to the buyer.

Tax ramifications

Before getting too deep into this part of the discussion, I want to strongly advise you to do one thing: Discuss your own tax liability, existing and potential, with your CPA or tax advisor. I hope that you have been keeping in touch with this person as you've moved through the project, but at this point, it is imperative that you talk with your tax advisor and provide him or her with all the information you have on the project from start to finish.

One thing you will want to discuss with your tax advisor is whether you have done this flip as an investment or whether this is a regular, ongoing business for you. In certain cases, an individual doing work as a continuing business can get certain extra deductions for which someone doing the work as an investment isn't eligible. However, merely deciding that you're doing this as a business won't get you that benefit. You must meet certain standards. Your CPA can advise you on whether you qualify.

If you are an investor, you may be able to pay tax on your profit as a capital gain, as opposed to regular income tax rates. This depends in large part on how long you've held the property. If you haven't held it for a long enough period since you first acquired it, you'll probably pay the higher income tax rate. Again, your tax advisor can point you in the right direction.

Finally, if you are going to try to defer paying any tax you owe by doing a 1031 Tax Free Exchange, you'll want your tax expert to very carefully advise you on how to do so. It's called a 1031 Exchange because that is the number of the section of the Federal Tax Code that permits this process. The reason is that to do a 1031 you must, among other things, purchase a replacement property for the one you are selling within a very specific period of time after you close on the one you're now selling. That period is 180 days from the close of the sale of the old property. If that isn't tough enough, you also have to identify the specific property you'll be buying within 45 days of closing your sale. One day off in either case and you destroy the exchange, thereby losing its benefits.

What benefits? You can defer the payment of your capital gains tax on the property for as long as you are invested in a succeeding property. In theory, if you follow one 1031 with another as you move from property to property, you never pay taxes until you finally cash out. If you die before cashing out, you owe no tax, and your heirs inherit the last property at its then current value, tax free. Again, however, I strongly recommend you talk to your tax advisor.

Sometimes a buyer will request a final walk-through to be sure that everything is as it's supposed to be. However, even if the buyer finds something amiss, it is not a valid reason to void the purchase. Any problems at this stage will have to be resolved after closing the transaction. Depending on the nature of the problem, this may be resolved in any number of ways, from simple negotiation and agreement to litigation. Hopefully, you won't have to worry about this. It is the exception, but it does happen. Other than that, you're basically done. You may personally give the key to the buyer, or have your agent arrange this. Some folks have a bottle of wine delivered to the address once the new owner has taken possession, but it's strictly a matter of choice.

 Moneysaver

You may be able to defer paying capital gains tax on your profits by virtue of doing a 1031 Exchange and placing your receipts into another property. Check with your CPA for details.

"Thank you, sir! May I have another?"

Well, you've done it. You've completed your project. I hope that it went as well as you'd planned, and you made as much profit as you'd hoped. Now, the question is: What do you do from this point? Do you start looking for another property to flip, perhaps going in a bit deeper than you did on this one? Maybe you just finished a cosmetic flip, and, since it went so well, you want to try your hand at an intermediate flip. Perhaps you did an intermediate flip, liked the

> 66 When you are done, beyond the financial rewards, you have the satisfaction of knowing that you've created something. You have made a silk purse out of a sow's ear, which is now someone's cherished home. That's very satisfying. 99
>
> —Robert, experienced flipper

challenge, and want to keep working at that level. Or maybe you're ready to challenge yourself with a total gut.

Maybe you've completed this venture and, upon reflection, feel that it was a good experience, but one that you'd like to step away from at least for the immediate future. Whatever choice you make, remember—look at all of the facts and then decide. Good luck!

Just the facts

- You'll handle all of the closing documents that effectively allow title to be passed from you to the buyer.

- A reconveyance from the lender removing your liability under a mortgage on the property will be forwarded to the county for recordation.

- Your CPA can help you receive the applicable benefits to reduce or defer your tax liability on the project's profits.

- Once you're done, you have a choice: Do another flip, or enjoy your success and move on to something else.

Glossary

agency The legal relationship between buyer or seller and their Realtor.

amortization The gradual repayment of a mortgage through monthly (for example, installment) payments over a fixed period of time.

appraisal The professional examination of property for the purpose of estimating the current market value or worth of a property. The written report of same.

brokers open A special open house usually restricted to Realtors to allow them the first opportunity to view new properties when they come to market.

CAMO The process by which a small group of Realtors will view a property with a goal of establishing a price for it.

closing statement A statement prepared by a title company giving a complete itemization of costs incurred in a real estate transaction. A separate statement is prepared for the buyer and seller.

cloud on title An issue about the legality of an owner's legal title to real property. It calls into question the legality of the owner's legal title. These can be removed only by a court action referred to as a "Quiet Title" action.

codes, covenants, and restrictions (CC&Rs) Rules set down limiting uses of and changes to property in a homeowners association. Also, may be found in condominium association owners groups.

comparables   *See* comps.

comps   Short for "comparables," these are similar properties to your flip in the same geographical area that either have recently sold or are currently on the market.

contingency   A condition in a contract that must be met for the contract to be binding; for example, inspection contingency or loan contingency.

curb appeal   The attractiveness in appearance of a home as first viewed from the street by potential buyers.

default   The action by a borrower failing to abide by the terms of a loan set by the lender when the loan was made. It is the first step in the foreclosure process. *See also* foreclosure.

disclosures   Information about a house and its surroundings being sold provided by the seller to buyers and potential buyers. Often, but not always, this is information that either is or may be perceived to be derogatory about the property or its surroundings.

double-paned windows   Windows with two panes of glass. These are better than single-paned windows for insulation. In colder climates, triple-paned versions are common.

earnest money   Deposit made when buyer makes an offer to buy property.

easements   A legal form of title to a property that allows its beneficiary to have access to or across a particular piece of real property. These are usually granted by the legal owner of the property to the benefited party, and, in most cases, continue in perpetuity.

entitlements   *See* permits.

escrow   The process used in many parts of the western United States to handle a sale of property. It involves a neutral party, often a title company, to handle all holding and exchange of money and documents related to a sale of real property. In other parts of the country, these items are usually handled with the assistance of an attorney.

flip The purchase of a house with the intent to fix it up or update it, then sell it for a profit. Depending on the degree of work, may be a "cosmetic," "intermediate," or "total gut."

For Sale By Owner (FSBO) Refers to real estate sold by the owner rather than with a Realtor representing the seller.

foreclosure The process by which a lender takes over possession and legal title to a property on which it has made a loan. The process commences when the borrower defaults and the lender formally records a "Notice of Default." After a statutorily mandated period of time, the property is sold at public auction with the lender receiving the proceeds up to the amount owed. If this amount is not realized during the bid, the property reverts to the lender. Foreclosure auctions can sometimes be an excellent place to acquire flippable property well below market value.

foundation The structural base of a home; it supports the rest of the structure and must be correctly sized to be able to support a certain sized structure. The larger the structure, the larger and thicker the foundation.

framing The vertical structure of a house consisting of vertical struts, usually wood or metal, and horizontal top and bottom pieces. It is to the framing that siding and sheetrock are later attached when enclosing a house. *See also* sheetrock.

grandfathering The process whereby situations that may violate current code or law are permitted to remain unchanged because those situations predated the current code. They were previously legal under pre-existing code.

home inspection service A service performed by a contractor or experienced individual or company; the purpose is to detect and diagnose defects in a property and generally evaluate its condition. It evaluates a property's structure and mechanical systems.

Internet   The World Wide Web, where all manner of subjects can be exposed to the view of potentially millions of people. It has become a major place to market real estate. *See also* Realtor.com.

keysafe   *See* lockbox.

lead paint disclosure   Federally mandated, this is the seller's disclosure of any known lead-based paint used in the house.

lien   The legal method for a creditor to place a claim on real property. These include mortgages, judgment liens, and mechanic's liens.

living area   Usually measured in square feet, this is the area inside a dwelling.

lockbox   Sometimes referred to as a keysafe, this is placed on the property for sale by the listing Realtor and contains a key to the property. It is accessible only to other Realtors.

lot site   The area of the lot where the house is located. It is commonly measured in either square feet or acres.

market absorption rate   The process by which a Realtor calculates how long it takes a real estate market to absorb all properties available for sale on that market at any given time. The longer this absorption period is, the slower the market and the more favorable to buyers it is.

marketing flyer   A paper flyer that features pictures and information on a house for sale.

mold   Fungal growth, caused by moisture. There are literally thousands of types, but a very few are highly toxic. Due to this, mold inspections are recommended if there has ever been a history of leaks or moisture in the home.

mortgage   Although most people refer to their loan to purchase real property as a "mortgage," actually the term refers to the legal document that the loan is based upon. In the early years of a mortgage, most of the monthly payment goes toward interest. Later in the mortgage, more of the payment goes toward reducing the loan's principal balance.

Multiple Listing System (MLS)   The system for all members of a local Board of Realtors to make their listings available to other Realtors and/or their clients.

multiple offers   The situation when more than a single offer is received from buyers for a piece of real property.

NAR   National Association of Realtors.

open house   Times hosted by listing Realtors to publicly display homes for sale to other agents and the public.

permits   Legal authorizations to the property owner for alterations to be made to the property.

purchase contract   The document between buyers and sellers of real property that specifies price and other terms of the purchase/sale of the property.

real property   Another term for "real estate." "Real property" is differentiated from "personal property," which is any property that is not real estate (such as a car and personal possessions).

Realtor.com   Web site of the National Association of Realtors (NAR); the largest real estate Web site.

return on equity   Also called return on investment (ROI), this is the percent gain on the amount of money a buyer receives on his or her investment when he or she sells it.

return on investment (ROI)   *See* return on equity.

sheetrock   Also known as wallboard, it is the most common material used today for interior walls. It replaces the form, lathe, and plaster used prior to the 1950s.

staging   The process of making a home and property for sale look as good as possible by expert use of furniture, accessories, and color/design.

title insurance   Provided by a title insurance firm, this insures the owner of real property against any claims against his or her legal title to the property. It is obtained when a buyer purchases a property, and usually also notes any exceptions that are not covered by the policy, as well as such things as easements on the property. *See also* easements.

title search   Detailed examination of the entire document history of a property title to make sure there are no legal encumbrances that affect the seller's right to sell. Done by the title insurance company before issuing title insurance. In states where attorneys handle real estate transactions, attorneys often perform this function.

Universal Resource Locator (URL)   The term referring to an Internet address.

variance   An exception to a particular code that is applied for by the property owner and either granted or denied by the applicable government authority. Most commonly, these are applied for when someone doing major work on a property wants to do something that is precluded by the applicable codes.

virtual tour   An electronically based series of photos of a property arranged in sequence to allow a distant viewer the opportunity to "tour" a property he or she may be interested in. These can be found on Realtors' Web sites, as well as on the local Multiple Listing System (MLS). They can also be e-mailed to interested potential buyers.

wallboard   *See* sheetrock.

zoning   The process by which cities and other governmental authorities limit certain types of property to specific areas of a town or city. For example, industrial properties can only be in one area, and retail in others.

Resource Guide

Here is just a sample of the resources out there for anyone interested in not only exploring the subject more in depth before taking the plunge, but also as sources of information while doing a flip.

Web sites

Don't forget to check the individual Web sites of local Realtors and brokerages. These will show what things are selling for locally.

ezinearticles.com

"A Beginner's Guide to Flipping Houses"
As the name suggests, it's a basic how-to Web article.

"Flipping Houses for Gold: Three Tips to Help You Find the Perfect Fixer"
Another e-zine article to use as a guide in starting flips.

BobVila.com

Bob Vila's Web site base to all of his home repair activities and shows.

Realtor.com

The largest real estate Web site in the world, it shows prices locally and nationally for property.

REIDepot.com

> A resource Web site that offers free blog articles, and "for sale" tapes, books, and other material on all aspects of real estate investment.

www.doghousetodollhousefordollars.com

> Informational site for info on flipping houses; must register to get some of the information.

www.Flipping-Houses.com.

> A paid-for, members-only site on real estate information; has some free downloadable books.

www.FreeRealEstateStrategies.com

> Free (for 6 months) real estate investment advice.

www.househunting101.com

> Blog publishing site that puts others' real estate-related blogs on the Web.

www.PropertyForeclosure.com

> Site selling methods to successfully invest in foreclosure properties.

www.realestatejournal.com

> Real estate information and news site run by *The Wall Street Journal.*

www.rehablist.com

> Access to "fixers," foreclosures, and "hard money" loans across the U.S.

www.USHUD.com

> Foreclosure list for possible flippable homes.

TV shows (check local listings)

Bob Vila's Home Again

Flip This House

This Old House

Computer programs

3D Home Architect by Broderbund. This simple but very useful CAD (computer aided design) program allows one to play around with rooms and space to come up with possibilities for the design. Unlike many CAD programs, it's very easy to use, and although the plans are not construction documents, they are extremely helpful.

Quicken by Intuit. A good program that allows you to establish and maintain your financial records. You can use it for just your flips or for all of your financial records. A compressed version, **Quickbooks,** is very helpful when you sit down at year-end with your accountant.

Recommended Reading List

If you're looking for more reading material about flipping houses and related subjects, these books and magazines are a good place to start.

Books

Corbett, Michael. *Find It, Fix It, Flip It!: Make Millions in Real Estate—One House at a Time.* Penguin Group, New York: 2006.

Editors of Sunset Books. *Basic Home Repairs.* Lane Publishing, Menlo Park, CA: 1971. (Sunset Books offer an entire range of good information on various aspects of working on a house.)

Hamilton, Gene, and Katie Hamilton. *Fix It and Flip It: How to Make Money Rehabbing Real Estate for Profit.* McGraw Hill, New York: 2003.

Litchfield, Michael W. *Renovation, Third Edition.* Taunton Press, Newtown, CT: 2006.

Myers, Kevin C. *Buy It, Fix It, Sell It: Profit!.* Dearborn Financial Publishing, Inc., Chicago: 1997.

New Remodeling Book. Better Homes and Gardens Books. Des Moines, IA: 1998.

Various authors. *How to Make Your Realtor Get You the Best Deal.* Gabriel Publications, Sherman Oaks, CA: various dates. (Select from among various locales.)

Whitman, Roger C. *More First Aid for the Ailing House.* McGraw
    Hill, New York: 1977.

Articles and magazines

Goforth, Alan. "The Flip Side of Real Estate." *Kansas City Star,*
    August 13, 2006.

Hoffman, Christina Spira. "Remodeling's Payoff." *Realtor* maga-
    zine, December 1, 2005.

Kim, Lauren. "Where Houses Are Selling And Where They Are
    Not." *The Real Estate Journal,* June 28, 2006.

Steiner, Christopher. "Diamonds in the Rough." Forbes.com,
    October 3, 2005.

Inspired House Magazine. Taunton Press, Newtown, CT.

Smart Choices for Your Home. Taunton Press, Newtown, CT.

The Best of Fine Homebuilding: Kitchen Remodeling Projects.
    Taunton Press, Newtown, CT.

Words of Wisdom

Whether you're new to flipping or an experienced flipper, it's always valuable to hear comments from people who have "been there." I asked a few people I have worked with who have done, or worked on, various numbers of flips for their ideas on particular issues in conjunction with the process. Here's what the experts had to say.

First impressions: using color

Megan is an expert on both the use of color in redoing houses, and on curb appeal and external presentation of the property. On the subject of color, she says that using a neutral external color such as tan, sand, taupe, beige with green tones, or lighter greens is a better way to go and will appeal to a broader potential audience than using a more brilliant shade. "Stay away from pinkish or fleshy undertones," she recommends.

Megan also cautions that colors used for trim should make the main color of the house look sharp, while remaining appropriate for the architectural style that is involved. For example, she likes to use green tones for a woodsy cottage-style house and warmer colors for a Mediterranean-style home.

Megan also feels that exterior colors should, with a few exceptions, be limited to two. One exception is the multicolor schemes often found on San Francisco's Victorian homes. The only other is in the case of accent colors. Here, Megan feels a third color should be limited strictly to the front door or shutters, and be a sharp contrasting color, such as red, dark green, or black.

Plantings and ornaments

When it comes to plantings and ornamentation, Megan has one guiding principle: Keep things as simple and uncluttered as possible. The view of the home shouldn't be covered or overwhelmed by the plants and trees around it. Trees that are too large should be thinned, while smaller trees or bushes that infringe on the view can be either trimmed back or replaced by less overwhelming specimens. "Overgrown plants can make a house look smaller and instill worry in the minds of buyers as to what problems the plantings may be hiding," she advises. "A beautiful yard attracts." Megan also recommends the use of plants for color, saying it "doesn't have to match the home's color, but will make it feel more welcoming." Mature healthy landscaping such as a large maple or redwood tree shouldn't be removed, she advises, just trimmed so it's "sculptured and clean."

She recommends that yard ornaments be kept to a minimum, leaving open space for the buyers to personalize their homes. Trellises and pergolas are okay as long as they are used just for additional architectural detail.

Megan cautions that special areas of concern such as connecting walkways, entryways, and garage doors should be kept as clean and open as possible. She also says to "spend money to make it look good" when discussing garage doors; to maximize the appearance of the front entryway, she highly recommends potted plants. Hardware and outdoor lighting fixtures should be matched to tie everything together.

Her final bit of advice may seem obvious, but it concerns features that are frequently mishandled: Keep design and trim as much in conformity as possible. Stay with the traditional details of a particular type of design. Her best examples of this are avoiding the use of brick for Mediterranean-style homes, or the use of Mexican pavers for the approaches to a Victorian home.

Financing

One of the most important members of your team is the person who gets you your financing. Since he or she deals regularly in the costs for money—what money costs you to borrow (interest, points, and fees)—he or she should also be someone you'd go to for advice in this area, as well as advice on the best way to meet your financing needs. Someone I use virtually exclusively, Alan, is a mortgage broker. I tell people that "if Alan can't help you, then you can't get a mortgage." But he does more than get a buyer a loan. He counsels and tries to help a buyer obtain the best overall financing deal, not merely the one with the lowest stated interest rate.

Alan advises that when choosing the best finance "product" you should check with your lender about which type will be the lowest *overall* cost, not just initial interest rate. Factor in any other fees, as well as whether the financing will allow you to expand the amount borrowed and final repayment period should you have delays or unexpected cost overruns beyond your contingency plans in your budget. Each change cost—how it is planned for and dealt with—can save you money.

Interest rates

Another area Alan recommends thoroughly discussing with your lender is fixed or floating rates. You can get a five-year fixed-rate loan, but you should make certain there's no prepayment penalty if you repay in one or two years. Noting that flipping "is a business like any other," Alan says your best deal may not be strictly the lowest rate, fixed or floating, but the one that allows you the most flexibility in keeping your outgoing cash flow as low as possible.

Establish and maintain a good lender relationship

Alan emphasizes the importance of having a good relationship with your lender, saying you "can be penny wise and pound foolish" trying to get the lowest-cost loans by going from lender to lender. A solid ongoing relationship with a lender is imperative, especially if you plan on doing more than one flip.

Alan also notes that some lenders will bend the rules or laws on loan qualification just to get your business or to help you "make it work." He cautions that this lender should be avoided, noting that "if you need to bend rules to make the deal fly, you probably should rethink going forward at all."

Confronting problems

Tami, a Realtor who regularly does everything from cosmetic flips to very involved intermediate flips, says the most important items to be sure of are that the house has adequate drainage, and that there's no dry rot or any form of pest infestation. She feels that these are the surest ways to undermine even the best of substructures for a home. Simple inspections can reveal any problems, and then the flipper can decide how and if he or she should proceed.

On cosmetic flips, Tami feels that the most important areas are the kitchen, baths, and outdoor living areas such as decks and patios. Regarding the latter, she says "people *love* the indoor/outdoor feel of a house."

Stretching a dollar

One thing Tami firmly believes in for intermediate flips, both for the impression they give and the money they save, are "Home Depot" kitchens. Noting that you can get a wonderful kitchen fully outfitted wholly at large home improvement stores such as Home Depot, Tami says that is definitely the best way to go in many cases. She notes, "You can build a whole house at Home Depot."

When talking about cosmetic flips, Tami feels you get the most for your money and the best return by making the home look as expensive as possible. This is achieved through a good use of paint, coupled with refinishing floors, upgrading doors and moldings, and making the landscaping look as good as your budget will permit. Tami is a strong believer in curb appeal and first impressions.

Christine, who specializes in intermediate flips, echoes these thoughts. She says that frequently you can make a home look high end without spending high-end money. At large home improvement stores, she notes, "you can get 'high-end' finishes at lower than what you'd expect to pay elsewhere." She also says there are many areas of a house where refacing can save you lots of money and gain high returns when you sell. A good example is the fireplace of a house, which she will reface with slate over deteriorated brick.

Knowing when to stay away

When deciding whether to proceed with a flip, Christine says that, aside from obvious factors such as major damage to the house, she notices how the neighborhood looks at first blush. If the neighbors have cars up on blocks in the front yard, grass that needs cutting, or other signs of lack of care, "it's very easy to pass" on a possible flip candidate.

Appearance can mean everything

While on the subject of curb appeal, Christine also says the appearance of the front of the house is paramount in making a good first impression on buyers to get them to want to look inside and consider buying. Once inside, she carries the first impression rule to its logical conclusion, noting that she feels staging is the best thing you can do, post-construction, to "make the house look as good as possible."

Focus on major structural issues first

Another point she makes is that in the overall scope of things, there are sometimes relatively minor issues that will crop up. These should not get too much of your concern because, as she notes, "Anything that can legitimately be covered by paint

should be." Christine believes, however, it is much more important to pay attention to significant items before anything else.
"Focus on major structural or construction issues first."

While you're in escrow

An escrow officer I know, Marie, says one excellent way to save
on closing costs is to be sure to order a binder for your title policy. The title company will charge you the full premium plus an
additional 10 percent to cover the binder. If you're wondering
how paying an extra 10 percent is saving money, the answer is
that when you sell the property, at any time up to two or three
years after buying it (check your title company for specifics), you
get the entire base policy refunded to you. Result: You've been
covered for a net cost of 10 percent of the regular premium.

The reason for this is simple. When you order the binder,
you have the full binding commitment of the title insurance
company to insure you against claims on your legal title. You just
haven't actually taken out a policy. Thus, when you sell the property, you're entitled to get a refund of the unused premium—
the money that was for the policy you never ordered or
possessed.

Before and After

The following photographs show a recent intermediate flip before the work and after the flip was finished and staged for sale. While the basic footprint of the home—three bedrooms and two baths—was unchanged, major work was done in the kitchen and baths, while the flooring in the living and dining areas was changed and the house was repainted. The rear yard was also re-soded and a sprinkler system was installed. What a difference!

Here's the house as it appeared before any work was done on it. This view shows the front of the house. (Photo courtesy of Christine Pang)

The house has been repainted a more neutral color, a large window has been added, and the entryway has been improved in this "after" shot. (Photo courtesy of Patrick Carney)

The back yard shows a poor lawn and nothing attractive. (Photo courtesy of Christine Pang)

The back yard after new sod and a sprinkler system were installed. Notice how the simple addition of shrubs and flowers adds to the beauty of this back yard. (Photo courtesy of Patrick Carney)

The living room area as it appeared when the flipper purchased the home. The floor is bare of any covering at all. (Photo courtesy of Christine Pang)

The same area after repainting, new flooring, the addition of a slate veneer on the fireplace, and the staging of the home for sale. Yes, this really is the same home! (Photo courtesy of Patrick Carney)

Index